The Daily Doz Catholic Parenting

Improving Your Catholic Parenting in 20 Minutes a Day

im Otremba, M.Div, M.S., LICSW
nd Maureen Otremba, M.A.

Contents

How to Use This Workbook

Before you dive into Chapter 1, let's take a moment to consider just what we mean by "Catholic parenting." How does "Catholic" parenting differ from any other kind of parenting?

For starters, we presume that Catholic parents are well connected to their faith home: that is, their parish. Catholic parents are exhorted at the Baptism of their child to make it their daily concern to raise their child in the Catholic faith. This involves weekly worship, prayer at home, and living a life centered on Gospel values. It is a sacred duty (and a tall order!), and none of us gets it right all the time. We hope that you will consider this book an invitation to become more immersed in the great riches of the Catholic faith which we share, particularly through involvement in your parish.

Furthermore, the parish experience is designed to assist parents in their sacred duty as the first teachers of their children in the faith. It does this by means of weekly liturgy (Mass), through faith formation programs like Vacation Bible School, religious education, sacramental preparation, children's Liturgy of the Word, youth group, and various activities geared toward service and the social development of the children and youth in the parish. Unfortunately, some parents connect with the parish only when it is time for their child to receive a sacrament (for example, First Eucharist or Confirmation). The fact that you are reading this book is a sign that you want to be more involved. We encourage you to make your faith a priority. God's abundant blessings await you!

A few notes of explanation are in order. First, this workbook is not intended to be a summary of the Catholic faith. While at times we quote the *Catechism of the Catholic Church* (and note the reference as CCC and the paragraph number) and mention practices common to the Catholic experience, we don't pretend to represent the full scope of what it means to be Catholic. (Hardly possible in a book this size!)

How to Use This Workbook *continued*

Second, we draw on our professional experiences of counseling, teaching, pastoral ministry, parish work, and conducting retreats to illustrate various points in these chapters. Names and certain details have been changed in order to safeguard privacy and confidentiality.

A Word About Special-Needs Parenting

While the contents of this workbook are fashioned with typically-developing children and youth in mind, it is possible to apply some of these strategies and pointers to a child with special needs. As parents of two children with special needs, we are familiar with the process of sifting through how-to books and applying what works to each child's situation. We encourage those parents who are in a similar situation to consider the contents here, use what is helpful, and lay aside what is not. And know of our prayers for you as you meet the special challenges of your call.

Where to Go From Here

We suggest that you begin by working through the first four chapters in chronological order, since they provide a foundation for the remainder of the book. From there, feel free to go to the chapter that interests you most or is most pertinent to your current parenting situation.

Lastly

Please know that all the while we have been writing and revising this text, we have been praying for you, the parents who will use this material. We fervently ask God to bless your holy calling as parents and to give you the tools—and the grace!—you need to be the best parents you can be to your children. May the Holy Family intercede for you, and may the Holy Spirit enflame your family with love and deep peace!

1

First Daily Dozen: Our Identity as Parents

"We are children of God." —Romans 8:16

Our preferred place to begin any conversation about parenting is to consider who we were before we took on this momentous role. For Catholic parents, the answer is found in our Baptism: the joyous occasion when our own parents presented us to the Lord and the faith community (or when we as adults came through RCIA) for inclusion into the family of God. On that day we became God's child, a very brother or sister to Jesus Christ. What an amazing reality!

But in the daily demands of our busy lives, this abiding truth can often go unnoticed. Or it becomes obscured by the identity our culture would rather assign to us: our profession or occupation, our relationships or social status, our possessions or our hobbies, or even our appearance. It is important to take the time to acknowledge who we are by virtue of our Baptism:

> We are "*citizens with the saints, and also members
> of the household of God.*" —Eph. 2:19

In other words, we are part of a great family of faith, supporting each other in prayer, presence, and witness. As Catholics, this means that our parish is our faith home, a place where we support others and are supported by them in this common journey of parenting, each as a beloved child of God.

One practice we've found helpful in keeping this identity in mind is what we call the "wake-up" prayer:

> In the morning, even before you get out of bed, place your hand on
> your heart and say, *"Dear God, thank you that you have adopted me, and
> I am your son/daughter! May I be the best son/daughter I can be today. Amen."*

It takes just a few seconds, but it can make all the difference in your approach to the people you encounter in your day, because you have remembered your fundamental relationship to God.

Another way to keep this identity in mind is to see your bath or shower as a reminder of your Baptism. As you step into the water, or as it comes streaming down on you, recall that it was through water that you became God's child.

Of course, the best way for us as Catholics to be reminded of our identity as sons and daughters of God is to participate in the Eucharist. It is interesting to note that there are three Sacraments of Initiation: Baptism, Confirmation, and Eucharist. Each of these solidifies us in our identity as God's children. But only one of them is repeated, and that one is Eucharist. Just as we need to be fed regularly, so also we need to be reminded regularly of the great identity we have as God's children. This happens when we come together as God's family at the Eucharist.

Before You Continue

1) When was the last time you reminded yourself that you are a child of God?

2) What is one way you can remind yourself each day of this great identity?

Because we are children of God, it is critical to ask how we view God. Many parents don't stop to think about this question very often. Yet it is an essential question when discussing Catholic parenting, because how we view God will either help or hinder our parenting.

There are a few "ground rules" when doing image-of-God work:

1) **There are rarely neutral images of God** (the majority of our images are either positive or negative).

2) **All of our images of God will somehow be incomplete on this earth**. This is because God's ways are not our ways, and yet Jesus loves us with an intimate, personal love. God is an ultimate mystery yet is revealed in the Person of Jesus Christ. In our human condition all of our images of God will somehow be incomplete.

3) **Our image of God helps or hinders our parenting**. If our primary image of God is one of relentless judge who "waits to catch us messing up," that can actually increase stress hormones and blood pressure, which will not help us to be calm parents. If, on the other hand, our primary image of God is one of love who seeks us out (e.g., the Book of Hosea, the Song of Solomon, and many other places in the Bible) this will have a dramatic impact on our day-to-day peace and therefore on peaceful parenting.

Many parents have a very difficult image of God because of past abuse. If this is true in your case, we are very sorry. Please know that any past abuse can be healed, and that none of your past abuse was from God. The abuse was from human free will and sin. God did not create sin; people did. We learn this in Genesis with the fall of Adam and Eve.

God can heal abuse, but it usually takes professional counseling or meeting with a gifted pastor. If you find yourself reading this and thinking you might need some healing from abuse, please don't delay in seeking help. God desires to bring abundant life in you (John 10:10) and desires to heal all your past abuse.

So what about you? What is your primary image of God? Take five minutes right now to write down some words that best describe the primary way you view God to be in relationship with you:

Now take a look at that list. Is it mostly positive? Mostly negative? A combination? Take some time to pray about your primary image of God and how it relates to your stress levels. For example, if most of your list is negative, it could be helpful to pray with and understand the following Scripture passages, because they can begin to heal your negative images of God. As your negative image of God heals, your parenting will start becoming more positive. Pray with these images and memorize them:

+ "We are children of God." (Romans 8:16)
+ "See what love the Father has given us, that we should be called children of God." (I John 3:1)
+ "Do not fear, for I have redeemed you; I have called you by name, you are mine." (Isaiah 43:1)
+ "No one shall be able to stand against you all the days of your life. As I was with Moses, so I will be with you; I will not fail you or forsake you." (Joshua 1:5)
+ "As a mother comforts her child, so will I comfort you." (Isaiah 66:13)
+ "Peace I leave with you; my peace I give to you . . . Do not let your hearts be troubled, and do not let them be afraid." (John 14:27)

If we believe we are truly children of God, this will have a deep impact on every aspect of our lives. Two additional specific areas we want to explore in this chapter are self-talk and trust. Both can impact our parenting positively or negatively, because they form our own concept as children of God. And how we see ourselves as children of God carries over into the parenting of our own children.

Self-Talk

As parents, we need to be careful how we talk to, and about, ourselves. Too many of us have developed the destructive habit of verbally or emotionally beating ourselves up with shame, which is never from God. It is interesting that both guilt and shame quote Scripture. Both tell us "we are sinners." The difference is that shame conveniently leaves out that we are **redeemed** sinners! That is a significant difference.

Healthy guilt tells me that I am a child of God, but that because I will make mistakes, I must confess them and I can be forgiven. Then, I can live more fully from my great identity as a child of God. Shame tries to convince me that I am unlovable and unforgivable, so therefore it is OK to verbally or emotionally berate myself.

Do you ever feel shame and verbally or emotionally beat yourself up?

Take some time right now to pray and think about that. If you beat yourself up with shame or other lies, write down how many times you criticize yourself emotionally or verbally every day, so you can begin to reduce that number.

Consider using the contract we've included on the next page. Remember, it takes about 60 days to develop a new action or attitude, so be gentle with yourself. If you use the contract, date it, because you can work on stopping this self-destructive behavior slowly. In a month, come back to it and see that you have learned new behaviors (telling yourself the truth of who you are as a child of God), instead of telling yourself any negative, shame-based lies.

Contract to Stop Negative Self-Talk

I think I verbally or emotionally scold myself _____ (fill in # times per day.) With God's grace and the Holy Spirit to help me, I will try today to reduce this number by one, until it's at zero, where God wants it. If needed I will wear a rubber-band around my wrist so if I catch myself starting to verbally or emotionally berate myself, I will gently "snap" myself back into the truth of who I am as a child of God! Or, I can simply put my hand on my heart and tell myself to treat myself as a child of God. Or, I will think about treating myself the way I would treat my best friend.

Instead of focusing on these shame-based lies, I will try to tell myself at least three Scripturally based realities of who I am in Christ (find them on page 9). I will sign and date this pledge and try hard today and in the future to stop any negative lies I say about myself. If I need to, I will copy this contract and put it up on my mirror, fridge, or any place I will see it daily.

Sign: _____ Date: _____

Child-Like Trust

Whereas self-talk can strengthen or weaken the realization of our identity, the ability to trust God in all aspects of parenting (and life) is a sign that we're secure in that identity.

Becoming more of who we are as children of God is not just some neat idea in a parenting workbook; it is a direct commandment from Christ! In the Gospel of Mark, Jesus tells us that unless we receive the Kingdom of God like a child, we will never enter it (Mark 10:15). This is a very challenging idea for us adults because we sometimes forget what it is to be child-like, and instead we become more childish by being self-absorbed or trying to depend too much on our own strength. Thank the Lord that we have our own children to remind us that fundamentally, a child-like heart trusts.

Before You Continue

1) When was the last time you acted more child-like by trusting that God will provide for your needs?

2) How can you replicate that idea in your life today and in the future?

Acquiring this child-like heart is essential, yet difficult. When the pressures of finances, relationships, work, life, or world situations weigh us down, it is good to remember that we are children of God. God calls us to trust in His divine mercy to transform our concerns and to help us to understand what we can and can't control.

Take some time to list the major worries that you feel right now:

Next, organize your worries into three categories:

1) Worries you can't control.
2) Worries you can directly control.
3) Worries you partially control.

For example, you may have "the economy" on your worry list. Consider: how much direct control do you have over the economy? Not much at all. Decide which other items you do not control and cross them off your list. As you cross them off the list, give yourself verbal permission to not worry about them today. Use the past tense to let these go: tell yourself "In the past I used to worry about you, but now I see that I have no direct control over you and so I will not worry about you today." Tell the worries in this category: "I need to save my energy for the next two categories; I don't have time for you anymore."

The more you tell yourself these messages, the more you will slowly start believing them and thereby evict this entire category from your thoughts.

It's easier said than done, but if it isn't said, it won't get done.

Now, we need to develop a working plan for the second and third categories (worries you directly control and worries you partially control). As Christians we know the Scriptural promise: "Cast all your anxiety on him, because he cares for you" (I Peter 5:7). In order to give our worries to God, it's essential to understand who we are as children of the King. Because we are children of God we have dominion (through Christ and the Holy Spirit) over these worries in our lives. With this power in mind, here are some ways that have helped us and other parents "give" these categories to God. You can re-write them and safely burn them, journal them out and shred them, pray them out, talk them out, or exercise them out (when you start to sweat think about harnessing the worry and using it up as "fuel" for your exercise). Select one that works for you and practice it today.

Before You Continue

Which ideas in this chapter did you like the best, and how can the Holy Spirit help you use those ideas in your Catholic parenting?

Prayer About Your Identity as a Child of God

All loving God, You have made me Your child, and You have good plans for me and my parenting. Send Your Holy Spirit and awaken within me the attitudes and actions I need to change today and so create the little church that You desire in my family. I ask this through Christ our Lord and in the power of Your Holy Spirit. Amen.

2

Second Daily Dozen: Our Children's Identity

"Let the little children come to me." —Mark 10:14

If we as parents are children of God, it only makes sense that our children are also primarily God's children as well. This is a profound truth in our lives: God trusts us so much that He allows us to co-create new children with Him. God creates the soul, and we "help" God create the body. Do you think of your children as God's children first? When we start to do this, a new respect and deeper love can take hold.

Once when Jim was praying with a family about this truth, Jack (the father of the family) said he felt challenged to treat his children better. Jim went on to pray that all parents could come to realize that the way we talk to our children or spouse is the way that we talk to Christ.

That prayer reminded Jack that Christ told His disciples, ". . . just as you did it to one of the least of these who are members of my family, you did it to me." (Mt. 25:40). Jack said he never thought of it that way. As he began trying to see his children as God's children first, he experienced a measure of healing in his relationship with his son. In fact, in his next session with Jim, Jack related that his son was hugging him more often because he was treating his son as Christ. That fruit was from realizing and practicing this Daily Dozen.

If our children are first God's unique children, then we are challenged to resist negatively comparing our children with their siblings or with other children. This is difficult to do in our competition-saturated culture. We use the word "negatively comparing" because we believe that some comparing is healthy and good. For example, we need to learn where our children are developmentally by comparing them with other children of the same age and ability. This is good and necessary. What can be damaging is when we compare for competition's sake.

We remember a time when Jim fell into this trap himself while our daughter was in an accelerated reading program in school. Our daughter devours books and does very well at school (okay—maybe we're biased). Of course, we think canceling the cable TV and monitoring her screentime has helped (more about that later). Suffice it to say, she is a good reader.

In this program the kids accumulate points based on what level of books they have read and their test scores. Jim remembers a conversation he had with her about her reading, and how he asked a competition-based question: "So honey, are you the top reader in your class?" "I don't know, daddy," was her child-like response, which reminded us that it doesn't matter if she is the top reader or not. In her innocence she didn't know if she was the top reader in her class, and she really didn't care . . . what a child-like heart and a great lesson for him as her daddy, who works with children as a therapist and should have known better. This challenged both of us to recognize that our children are first God's children, and so we don't need to compare them to any other child. God doesn't compare us with anyone else, and neither should we as parents.

One practice we recommend to all families is to have on every mirror of their house this simple, yet powerful, phrase: "I am a child of God. Treat me lovingly." When our children are too young to write this, we as parents can write it for them so that they grow up seeing that sign and internalizing this empowering truth.

If you're reading this and you don't have this sign up in your house, it's not too late to start. If your children are old enough to make the sign themselves, let them—it can create a sense of ownership. Even teens need to know this truth, and perhaps they can make it on the computer and print it out. (As an aside, teens usually prefer not to be referred to as a child, so they can write: "I am a son/daughter of God; treat me lovingly.") Either way, this truth is powerful, as we have seen over the years.

Once during one of Jim's Daily Dozen parenting workshops, a mom told the group that she had purchased the book and started working through the content. She then shared with the whole church this story:

The couple has three children: two daughters and a son. One day, the then-nine and 10-year-old daughters were arguing and the seven-year-old son came up to them and said, "Um, excuse me, are you treating each other as daughters of God?" That true story shows the power of this little yet significant practice of putting these signs up on the mirrors in the bathroom so that our children can be soaked each day in this truth. This truth can change our lives!

Before You Continue

1) Are there times when you negatively compare your child or children to their siblings or to other children? What is the cause of this comparison?

2) When you look at your children, do you remember who they are primarily as God's children? What qualities of God do you see in them?

3) Do you have your great identity reminders up where you'll see them?

Write out who you are as a child of the King and post it on your mirror, cell phone, smartphone, computer, "pop-up" windows, etc. to remind you who you are as a child of God.

Prayer About Our Children's Identity

All gracious God, You have created all of us in Your image and likeness, and You dwell in our hearts. As I talk to my child today, give me the grace to know that I am addressing Christ. May my words be kind, and my actions be loving so as to build up this little Christ You allow me to nurture. In the power of the Holy Spirit, and through Christ our Lord, I pray. Amen.

3

Third Daily Dozen: Some of What We Need

"Come away to a deserted place all by yourselves, and rest a while."
—Mark 6:31

It's an impossible task to list here all that we as parents need. But we believe the conversation has to start with the wisdom from Jesus in the Gospel of Mark when He tells His loved ones to rest. We need rest! The placement of our needs before our children's needs is intentional. If our needs as parents are not met, then we can't even begin to meet our children's needs. This is illustrated in an encounter Jim remembers with a client we'll call Angie.

Angie came into Jim's office in tears and nearly hysterical. She told him, with anger and frustration, that she was at the end of her rope, that being a mom and a wife just wasn't working anymore, and that she wanted to "run away." Jim built rapport with her and listened to her story, which was laden with cries of hopelessness.

By the end of the session she felt a little better, having dumped all her stress out on a trusted person (her counselor, Jim). Over the course of her treatment she and Jim decided that as a mom and wife she had forgotten about a very important person in the mix: herself. They worked hard at creating new assertive boundaries so that she learned how to say that beautiful word we love to teach (a word we both learned from our own parents): "No." They also worked on helping her to rest, as our Lord teaches.

Through the Holy Spirit working in their relationship, Angie found a new understanding of who she is as a precious and powerful daughter of the King. She made more time for herself. She and her family and marriage are much better now, thanks to God. Her story is typical of many parents in our society. We're all working so hard as parents, spouses, friends, church members, and citizens that we often forget about ourselves and our needs and cares.

In order to avoid burn-out as parents, we need to think about what we can do to take care of ourselves based on examples from Christ's life. At times when we discuss making time for ourselves as parents, we encounter the objection that this is a "selfish" thing to do. After all, Christ died for us; can't we just "offer it up" and check our attitude?

Our response is that before Christ died for us, He lived for us. He lived fully, taking the necessary time for daily activities in order to accomplish the Father's will. Do we think we or our needs are any different?

As parents, we have many needs, and we don't need to feel guilty about making time for them. The four needs we want to focus on in the rest of this chapter are based on Christ's life. He had a need for prayer, staying para-sympathetically dominant through life (we'll explain), life-giving relationships, and exercise. We who call ourselves His followers need to follow His divine—and very human—example.

Our Need for Prayer

Often in the Gospel we see Christ leaving His friends and followers to be alone in order to spend time with His Father, whom He called "Abba" (or "Daddy"). He has left us a supreme example in this. In the midst of His ministry activities He would leave. He could have been healing someone, raising someone from the dead, forgiving someone, or a variety of ministry activities . . . but He chose to leave. Did He make a mistake? Hardly! He knew the centrality and importance of prayer. Likewise, we need to create time in our busy lives as parents to follow His lead for daily prayer.

Prayer is critical in our Christian parenting. Without prayer we can't respond to God's intimate and infinite love. It is only through prayer that we are able to graciously receive Abba's love for us through Christ so that we can lavishly share that love with our family and the world! It is only through prayer that we can receive and return the bountiful fruits of the Holy Spirit listed in Gal. 5:22 - 23: love, joy, peace, patience, kindness, goodness, self-control, faithfulness, and gentleness.

What is prayer? There are many types of prayers. Let's look at several different types through the acronym "PRACTICE." We benefit from thinking about and practicing these prayer forms in our lives and our parenting. (see the next page.)

"Practice"

P = Petition is asking for something or praying for someone else.

R = Repentance is turning away from sin and turning to God. We celebrate repentance in the Sacrament of Reconciliation.

A = Adoration is praise and worship. Our Catholic tradition places a special emphasis on praying before the Blessed Sacrament, and some parishes have even become centers of perpetual adoration, where the Blessed Sacrament is exposed for adoration at all hours in a special chapel. Adoration can also take the form of listening to Christian music or even glorying in nature and thanking God for creating everything!

C = Contemplation is thinking about or reflecting on a word or phrase from Scripture. This is part of the time-honored Catholic approach to Scripture called *lectio divina* (Latin for "divine reading). Consider using one of the many good resources available for praying with Scripture, such as *Magnificat* or *Give Us This Day*. For more on this prayer form, see ocarm.org/en/content/lectio/what-lectio-divina.

T = Thanksgiving. Thanking God for all God has done is essential! Ideally, our parenting and our lives should be one of thanksgiving! In fact, the word "Eucharist" *means* "thanksgiving."

I = Individual devotions hold a treasured place in the rich Catholic tradition and include the Rosary, novenas, traditional prayers such as the Chaplet of Divine Mercy, calling on the saints for their intercession, and First Friday devotion to the Sacred Heart of Jesus, just to name a few.

C = Communal prayer. We cannot be Catholics apart from a community. God desires that we worship at Mass every week and on Holy Days. Other forms of communal prayer include the Liturgy of the Hours, prayer vigils for special occasions, and Communal Penance Services. Each of these is an opportunity to gather as the Body of Christ in our common worship of God and in prayer for each other.

E = Experiential is praying through your experiences of everyday life: "So whether you eat or drink, or whatever you do, do everything for the glory of God" (1 Cor. 10:31). This is the "holiness of the humdrum" that's so necessary in our parenting. Doing dishes for the eighth time in a day is really an opportunity to lift it up as a prayer!

Before You Continue—Prayer Forms

1) What types of prayer feed you most?

2) How can you make time in your day for prayer?

3) What is God calling you to do today to meet your needs as a parent?

Before You Continue—Experiential Prayer

1) What activities will you do today that you can lift up to God as prayer?

2) For whom will you pray?

3) How can doing your daily tasks for the Lord bring new meaning to your list of parental activities that must be completed?

Staying Para-Sympathetically Dominant Throughout Life

The Psalmist says, "I am fearfully and wonderfully made!" (Ps. 139:14). Indeed, we are. The Lord has blessed His crown of creation, the human race, with an incredible mind, body, and soul.

Before we briefly describe how stress is inevitable, but anxiety is optional, it's good to recognize that graduate courses are taught on these biological systems. It's far beyond the scope of this workbook to go into depth on these systems. Yet it's helpful to have a basic understanding of these miracles that we sometimes take for granted.

Before the fall of humanity described in Genesis 3, it's reasonable to believe that we had no stress or anxiety. But after the fall we can't escape the reality of stress. Even the beginning of our life is stressful.

When the egg and sperm meet and create a new person, the resulting individual immediately and automatically creates a hard "shell" so no more sperm can enter in: the stressful reality of protection. Stress happens at a cellular level when our cells divide for the first time and slowly begin to create new organs and systems. These are examples of "good" stress: stress that's needed for us to grow and be protected. There's also toxic stress that happens at a biological level when a virus or bacteria invade, trying to wreak havoc. Because stress is everywhere, God has given us an intricate system to help us maintain our balance in stressful times.

This system that God gives us helps us to excel or know when we're in trouble. It's a division of the autonomic nervous system called the sympathetic nervous system (SNS). The SNS is a vast network that helps us move, think, feel, and even perform to the highest of our abilities (the "peak-performance" of the SNS). When athletes are "in the zone," the "zone" is the silent miracle we call the SNS.

But, like all things God created, there's a sacred order implicit in this division of the autonomic nervous system. And like most difficulties, problems start developing when we're out of balance and the sacred order that God intended breaks down. This lack of balance happens when the SNS goes beyond its peak performance and no longer is in regulation with the "counterpart" of the SNS. The "counterpart" of the SNS is called the para-sympathetic nervous system (PSNS). The PSNS is critically important for balance; it's the "rest and digest" part of the nervous system.

Here's an easy way to remember the difference between these two miracles: the sympathetic nervous system (SNS) starts with an "S," and so does the word "stress." Likewise, the word "para-sympathetic nervous system" (PSNS) starts with a "P," just as the word "peace" does. It's no coincidence that the Lord leaves His peace to us during the Last Supper in the Gospel of John. Jesus tells his apostles, and us, "Peace I leave you, my peace I give to you" (John 14:27). Jesus—the great healer—tells us that He wants us to be in total balance, in right relationship, with Abba, Himself, the Spirit, and others. This right relationship is maintained by the para-sympathetic nervous system.

When we're fresh from God at birth, we naturally understand this! Unless an infant is born to a mother using too many drugs, or the baby has medical conditions, a newborn understands in her body how to stay para-sympathetically dominant. Consider that when you were a newborn, you came into this world with the innate ability to breathe deeply. These deep diaphragm breaths helped keep you para-sympathetically dominant! This is just one of the many profound lessons that newborns teach us.

This ability to breathe deeply helps the newborn stay balanced. But then life happens. Stress happens, and we forget how to stay balanced and get stressed out. Our parents might yell at us (raising our cortisol levels—and triggering our sympathetic nervous system), or we grow up thinking we have no control over anxiety. We forget the lesson we knew in our bodies as infants, and we no longer breathe from the diaphragm. This lack of deep breathing, as well as other essentials to stay calm, can lead to our being sympathetically dominant in our lives, which increases our stress.

When we stay in the sympathetic nervous system too long, it can lead to anxiety. That's why we say that stress is inevitable, but anxiety is optional. For those who wrestle with anxiety, it doesn't feel "optional." But the truth is, for those of us who were not born with major difficulties, we innately knew how to stay balanced as a newborn.

This para-sympathetic dominance is then lost as we slowly get out of the practice of balance. The more balance we have, the more para-sympathetically dominant we are, just as we were when we were born. Stress will continue in our lives, and some of it will be toxic, but as long as we practice ways to stay in balance, that stress doesn't have to lead to anxiety.

One of the keys to making sure our stress doesn't lead to anxiety is to create daily habits that will keep us para-sympathetically dominant. For more truths and tips on staying para-sympathetically dominant, check out our workbook for Christian stress management: *A New Day in Christ: Calming Stress and Anxiety in 20 Minutes a Day*. Order it through our website: www.coachinginchrist.com or through Amazon.com.

Our Need for Life-Giving Relationships

There are, of course, many more needs that we have as parents, especially the need for life-giving relationships with members in the Body of Christ. We are not transformed in a vacuum. We need healthy interdependent relationships so that we are able to become more and more of who we are as children of God. Christ had three close, intimate friends while on this earth. Count yourself blessed if you have two or three as well. We don't need many, but we need a few.

The forms that these life-giving relationships take will depend on our needs as a parent. If there are significant areas in your life that need healing (depression, anxiety, emotional eating, unhealed past abuse, etc.) you may need a healing relationship to respond to that need.

Jim remembers working with Jan a few years ago. Jan was a stay-at-home mom, a wife, and a very faithful Catholic. It took her years to finally see that she needed a healing relationship in her life in order to work on past wounds. When she did come in for Christian counseling he recalls her saying, "Jim, I thought prayer and time alone with God would be enough to heal the past . . . why wasn't it enough?" He looked at her and told her that the wounds happened in relationship so therefore the healing needed to happen in relationship, too. She agreed and the Lord used their relationship to bring a good measure of healing from the past.

Healing relationships can be formed with your pastor or another priest, the pastoral minister in your parish, a Christian counselor or another qualified professional. Sometimes these relationships are with friends or coworkers who have the gifts of listening and affirming. Healing relationships are critical in life, and we should to pray about our need for them.

Before You Continue—Life-Giving Relationships

1) Do you need a healing relationship in your life?

2) In what areas of your life might the Lord be inviting you to do some healing work?

There are two good resources for locating a Christian therapist: www.family.org or www.aacc.net (American Association of Christian Counselors). If you seek a specifically Catholic therapist, your pastor or your Diocesan Office of Marriage and Family Life are good resources for referrals.

Once there has been some good healing work done in your life, you may seek life-giving relationships of a different form, such as a mentor from church, a friend who can hold you accountable, a spiritual director, or a Christian coach.

Note that there's a slight difference among mentoring, spiritual direction, and Christian coaching. All three are about transformation in the Holy Spirit through a trusted relationship, but they each have their own distinct flavor.

Mentoring is the most directive of the three. In a mentoring relationship there is an understanding that the mentor is a more "mature" Christian and that the person seeking mentoring needs to learn from the mentor. This is different from spiritual direction and Christian coaching.

In both coaching and spiritual direction there is no "mentor" per se. Instead of learning from a "mentor," there is a process of learning with another trusted person in the Body of Christ. Of course, it is important to choose spiritual directors and coaches based on their experience, training, and wisdom, but fundamentally these relationships are about journeying with another person in a non-directive way to discern together how God is working in a person's life.

Remember Jan, whom we discussed earlier in this chapter? She is seeing a spiritual director and is doing well. The healing work that she did in counseling laid the groundwork for more transformation in her life.

In the same way that we encourage others to do so, we both rely on our spiritual directors to help us keep perspective on our parenting. We thank God for the spiritual fruit we see from these life-giving relationships.

Our Need for Exercise

The last need that we will address in this section is exercise. Christ left us this example by the way He led His life; we sometimes don't think about that enough.

Both of us had the blessed opportunity to study in Israel while in graduate school, and we walked nearly everywhere. Walking up and down those hills of our Lord's land put most of us in excellent shape. Walking was Christ's main form of exercise, and if we learned from that example we could transform our relationships and our bodies.

Along with Christ's healthy diet, He was a good steward of His body; we need to make time to do the same.

Unfortunately, in our current culture, much of the activity that used to provide daily exercise, such as chores, farm work, skilled labor, and other manual work, has been taken over by machines, leaving us as a predominantly sedentary society (that is, we sit most of the time). This reversal makes it especially important for us to intentionally opt for physical activity in the form of exercise or other movement in order to stay healthy.

Walking is an excellent form of exercise. Simply walking three to four times a week for 30 minutes can do wonders for your health. *The Journal of the American Medical Association* concluded that the average pedometer wearer increased their daily walking by more than 2,000 steps a day (about one mile). Many smartphones have built in pedometers, or they cost about $15. You are worth that!

Often as parents we can feel as though we don't have time to exercise. But when we consider that we make time for what we value, it becomes a matter of priorities. Recently Maureen experienced this when she took our daughter Stephanie to sign up for membership at a local gym. Since Stephanie was too young to drive at the time, it occurred to Maureen that since she'd be driving Stephanie to the gym for training and workouts, it made sense for both of them to join the gym. This resulted in training sessions and regular workouts for both of them. Maureen describes the experience as "almost indulgent—taking time just for me and my health." She notes a higher level of energy, better moods, more restful sleep, and an increased sense of harmony and well-being. The truth is illustrated well here: when we take the time to meet some of our own needs, we in turn have the internal resources to meet the needs of others.

Before You Continue—Exercise

1) What is a roadblock to your making more time to exercise? How can you address it?

2) What connections can you see between exercise and prayer?

3) Perhaps you spend enough time exercising but need more alone or quiet time with the Lord. What is the Spirit calling you to do about your unmet needs as a parent?

Before You Continue

1) What was the most helpful information for you in this chapter?

2) How can this information help transform your parenting?

Prayer About Our Needs as Parents

All loving God, You created me in love and created me for love. Help me to learn from Christ's life so that I can tend to my parenting needs without guilt. Please send Your Spirit into my heart. Empower me to devote time for prayer, exercise, and life-giving relationships. I ask this through Christ our Lord and in the power of the Holy Spirit. Amen.

4

Fourth Daily Dozen:
Some of What Our Children Need

". . . do not provoke your children, or they may lose heart."
—Colossians 3:21

Just as it is difficult to list all the things we need as parents, it's also equally challenging to compile an exhaustive list of things that our children need from us. So we'll begin this chapter with a gentle "warning label": what our children need is nearly endless, and it seems like this chapter might be shame based. That is certainly not our intent. Rather, these reflections on what our children need fundamentally involve remembering who we are as children of God. While you are reading this material, please remember who you are as a child of God and how God is well-pleased with your great identity. If there are any actions or attitudes that this section challenges in your family, our prayer is that the Holy Spirit will use that challenge to breathe new life into your family and into your parental attitudes and actions.

Our Children's Needs by Age

Our children's needs vary depending on their ages and stages. Children go through relatively predictable stages of development based on their ages. Having a basic knowledge of these stages can help us be the best Catholic parents we can be by responding to what our children need during each stage.

This is just a quick glance into a broad topic. We encourage all parents to learn as much as possible when it comes to ages and stages.

We all make mistakes with every age and stage because none of us is perfect. But understand there's great hope based on the Holy Spirit's power working through "neuroplasticity"—the fact that our brain can continue to make great, healing connections throughout life! God is a good maker.

Pregnancy

Congratulations on your new baby! This is an incredibly exciting time for any parent. As Catholics, we hold the sacred belief that life starts at conception. So, even though the "name" of the human being might differ depending on its stage (blastocyst, fetus, newborn, toddler, tween, teen, adult, senior citizen), they are all human beings, because God creates the individual soul when the egg and sperm cell meet.

While you're pregnant, devote time to talk to your baby, pray with your baby, and bond with your baby. Soon your baby will be on the outside, and if you have been talking to him or her, your voice will be soothing as they go through the very difficult transition of birth.

Here is some information from the U.S. National Library of Medicine to help us understand the development of our babies:

Weeks 1-2

• The first week of pregnancy starts with the first day of a woman's menstrual period. She is not yet pregnant.
• During the end of the second week, an egg is released from an ovary. This is when you are most likely to conceive.

Week 3

• During intercourse, sperm enter the vagina after the man ejaculates. The strongest sperm will travel through the cervix (the opening of the womb, or uterus), and into the fallopian tubes.
• A single sperm and the mother's egg cell meet in the fallopian tube. When the single sperm enters the egg, conception occurs. The combined sperm and egg is called a zygote.
• The zygote contains all of the genetic information (DNA) needed to become a baby. Half the DNA comes from the mother's egg and half from the father's sperm.
• The zygote spends the next few days traveling down the fallopian tube. During this time, it divides to form a ball of cells called a blastocyst.
• A blastocyst is made up of an inner group of cells with an outer shell.
• The inner group of cells will become the embryo. The embryo is what will develop into your baby.
• The outer group of cells will become structures, called membranes, which nourish and protect the embryo.

Week 4

• Once the blastocyst reaches the uterus, it buries itself in the uterine wall.
• At this point in the mother's menstrual cycle, the lining of the uterus is thick with blood and ready to support a baby.

Week 5

• Week 5 is the start of the "embryonic period." This is when all of the baby's major systems and structures develop.
• The embryo's cells multiply and start to take on specific functions. This is called differentiation.

Weeks 6-7

• Arm and leg buds start to grow.
• Your baby's brain forms into five areas. Some cranial nerves are visible.
• Eyes and ears begin to form.
• Tissue grows that will become your baby's spine and other bones.
• Baby's heart continues to grow and now beats at a regular rhythm.
• Blood pumps through the main vessels.

For the rest on these stages, visit: www.nlm.nih.gov/medlineplus/ency/article/002398. htm

Newborn Babies

Congratulations on your new baby! Your baby is a precious gift from God, and yet having a newborn can (and has) put tremendous stress on the marriage (or on the single parent). If you are married, stay highly intentional of your spouse's needs and adopt a prayerful attitude to be marriage-centered while tending to the needs of your newborn. All of this takes prayer and priorities. Keep Christ in the center and life will be so much better.

Recent information suggests that we can predict with some accuracy if a new baby will attach and bond with his parents based on how the new parent bonded with their own parents. Babies need loving touch to bond!

Newborn babies need to be loved and their needs tended to with patience. You can't spoil a newborn. They need one-on-one touch and cuddle time with a loving parent who speaks gently to them. We love newborn babies because they invite us to ponder God's unconditional love and care for us. Try hard not to yell, because it can raise the baby's cortisol level, a stress hormone—too much and it causes the baby to become more agitated through the "anger center" of the brain (the amygdala). Newborns really do need tender loving care.

The newborn age and stage is "time out of time" partly because of the physical exhaustion that goes with it. However, God's love for us is more powerful than our physical tiredness. We need to pray for grace to be attentive to the many needs of these precious gifts from God.

Because the brain of a newborn is growing so rapidly and making new connections, every expert agrees that there should be absolutely no screentime for babies younger than two years of age. We need to get the word out about this!

Newborn babies need time to look into the face of a loving parent who picks up on the cues of their baby. When your baby is sympathetically dominant (review our past information on para-sympathetic dominance, if needed) and stressed out, the loving parent will pick up on those cues and try not to excite the baby anymore. Your baby's cue may be simply not "playing" anymore or looking away or crying. The more we attend to the baby's balance levels of stress and act on that positively, the more trust we are teaching our newborn.

In *Why Love Matters: How Affection Shapes a Baby's Brain* (Routledge, 2009), Dr. Sue Gerhardt states that the newborn "coordinates his system with those of the people around him. Babies of depressed mothers adjust to low stimulation and get used to a lack of positive feelings. Babies of agitated mothers may stay over-aroused and have a sense that feelings just explode out of you" (p. 37). In other words, our babies learn how to regulate the balance of either being sympathetically dominant or not from interacting with us.

Toddlers (the "Terrific Twos") (approx. 18–36 months). We prefer talking about the "terrific twos." Children this age are incredibly curious and love to explore. They need to explore but they also need to know that they are loved through positive prayer, talk, and touch.

Toddlers are in a natural stage of differentiation; they're figuring out that they are not you. This can be very exciting and very scary at the same time. As loving parents, we want to continue to love and connect with them gently, trying hard not to raise our voices, since this raises the stress hormone cortisol. As with newborns, too much cortisol will cause your toddler to become more agitated through the "anger center" of the brain (the amygdala) and act out negatively even more. It's ironic that the "go-to" response that most parents used with children of our generation to get them to behave (yelling) actually had the opposite effect, from a biological standpoint.

Try to change the environment—not your toddler. Your toddler's job is to explore, and certainly they do not have anything resembling an "adult brain" of reason. They're trying to figure out their world through exploration. It makes no sense to exhaust yourself saying "No!" to a toddler five times in a row when the problem could be solved by changing the environment and making sure the child is in a room that is toddler-friendly to explore. Yes, this takes work, but it helps our toddlers understand that they're not the problem, and that this is a safe world, redeemed by Jesus.

Toddlers do better when they know what's coming in the immediate future (i.e. the next few minutes). Set a buzzer and tell them, "When the buzzer goes off, we will clean up the toys and get ready for supper." Or, "When the buzzer goes off, we are going to get in the car, fasten our seat belt and go see grandma." Use distraction with toddlers and make them laugh! This works very well for redirecting behaviors.

Pray with your toddler and read Bible stories every day! They need to know that Jesus loves them, and they need to know that God is safe. Who is their image of God? Their parents! All the more reason to understand our own needs and to approach our toddlers as calmly as possible so we can all stay parasympathetically dominant.

These calming behaviors teach them that God is a God of peace, and Jesus means it when He says "Be not afraid!" When we talk calmly to our toddlers and resist yelling at them, they learn to be calm and peaceful in their lives.

We do need to teach our toddlers that we don't throw things, we don't bite people, we don't hurt people or animals, and other limits. When they do these behaviors remind yourself that they are still learning, take a deep breath, say the "Don't Yell" prayer (see page 52) and simply say "We don't do that. You need to say 'I'm sorry'." Then, offer your toddler a "time-out," either on your lap or in their bedroom. Stay calm through these years by making sure your needs are being met.

Preschoolers (3–5 years old): a great age of curiosity, cuteness, and cuddling! Praise the Lord!

Some of what preschoolers need in our Catholic homes:

First and foremost, they need for us to attend to their spiritual necessities. These include daily prayer with their parents, including stories from a children's Bible, and exposure to good Christian music to help them learn about God's love for them (we recommend CatChat and the group Go Fish). These factors will make weekly Mass attendance more peaceful for your own family and for the people around you. Contrary to the opinion of some, children this age can and should attend Mass. They need to learn that weekly Mass is a priority for the whole family and that they can behave for an hour. Of course, certain measures must be taken to ensure their good behavior (e.g. they should be well-rested, know what expectations are, etc.). But for the vast majority of children who are already familiar with prayer in the home, behavior at church isn't an issue.

In addition, children this age need limited screentime that is carefully monitored and safe from scary, disturbing, and inappropriate images and themes. We highly recommend video series such as "Adventures in Odyssey" and "Veggie Tales." Conversely, we discourage most of what is on network television, as it is routinely populated by disrespectful children and adults and tends to promote a highly consumeristic mentality. Obviously, this caution applies to all children (and adults, too!).

Our children also need a stable environment, as free from yelling as possible. This requires us to be gentle with them and not to raise our voices. As we've mentioned, raised voices contribute to heightened cortisol levels, which over time will work against us by training their brains to go quickly to their anger center. Therefore, we as parents need to keep our tones and volumes at a healthy level.

Children also need responsibility for some appropriate tasks so they can learn that they are an important part of our family team (e.g. Clean up one mess before you start another). And they need to acquire a healthy Christian sexuality (see Chapter 8).

What a typical 3-year old can do:

The following information was obtained from www.cdc.gov/ncbddd/actearly/milestones/

Social and Emotional
- Copies adults and friends
- Shows affection for friends without prompting
- Takes turns in games
- Shows concern for a crying friend
- Understands the idea of "mine" and "his" or "hers"
- Shows a wide range of emotions
- Separates easily from Mom and Dad
- May get upset with major changes in routine
- Dresses and undresses self

Language/Communication
- Follows instructions with 2 or 3 steps
- Can name most familiar things
- Understands words like "in," "on," and "under"
- Says first name, age, and sex
- Names a friend
- Says words such as "I," "me," "we," and "you" and some plurals (cars, dogs, cats)
- Talks well enough for strangers to understand most of the time
- Carries on a conversation using 2 to 3 sentences

Cognitive (learning, thinking, problem-solving)

- Can work toys with buttons, levers, and moving parts
- Plays make-believe with dolls, animals, and people
- Does puzzles with 3 or 4 pieces
- Understands what "two" means
- Copies a circle with pencil or crayon
- Turns book pages one at a time
- Builds towers of more than 6 blocks
- Screws and unscrews jar lids or turns door handle

Movement/Physical Development
- Climbs well
- Runs easily
- Pedals a tricycle (3-wheel bike)
- Walks up and down stairs with one foot on each step

What a typical 4-year old can do:

Social and Emotional
- Enjoys doing new things
- Plays "Mom" and "Dad"
- Is more and more creative with make-believe play
- Would rather play with other children than by himself
- Cooperates with other children
- Often can't tell what's real and what's make-believe
- Talks about what she likes and what she's interested in

Language/Communication
- Knows some basic rules of grammar, such as correctly using "he" and "she"
- Sings a song or says a poem from memory such as the "Itsy Bitsy Spider" or "The Wheels on the Bus"
- Tells stories
- Can say first and last name

Cognitive (learning, thinking, problem-solving)
- Names some colors and numbers
- Understands the idea of counting
- Starts to understand time
- Remembers parts of a story
- Understands the idea of "same" and "different"
- Draws a person with 2 to 4 body parts
- Uses scissors

- Starts to copy some capital letters
- Plays board or card games
- Tells you what he thinks is going to happen next in a book

Movement/Physical Development
- Hops and stands on one foot up to 2 seconds
- Catches a bounced ball most of the time
- Pours, cuts with supervision, and mashes own food

What a typical 5-year old can do:

Social and Emotional
- Wants to please friends
- Wants to be like friends
- More likely to agree with rules
- Likes to sing, dance, and act
- Shows concern and sympathy for others
- Is aware of gender
- Can tell what's real and what's make-believe
- Shows more independence (for example, may visit a next-door neighbor by himself [adult supervision is still needed])
- Is sometimes demanding and sometimes very cooperative

Language/Communication
- Speaks very clearly
- Tells a simple story using full sentences
- Uses future tense; for example, "Grandma will be here."
- Says name and address

Cognitive (learning, thinking, problem-solving)
- Counts 10 or more things
- Can draw a person with at least 6 body parts
- Can print some letters or numbers
- Copies a triangle and other geometric shapes
- Knows about things used every day, like money and food

Movement/Physical Development
- Stands on one foot for 10 seconds or longer
- Hops; may be able to skip
- Can do a somersault
- Uses a fork and spoon and sometimes a table knife
- Can use the toilet on her own
- Swings and climbs

Elementary School Years (6–9 years old)

Some of what 6–9 year olds need in our Catholic homes:

In addition to the needs listed for younger children, such as daily prayer, weekly participation in Mass, a low-stress environment (low volume and no tones), and appropriate music and media, children this age have the following needs:

- They need more age-related responsibilities and maybe a "chore list" of things they need to do daily (clean room, dust, vacuum for a 9 yr. old, etc.).

- Leverages can work very well with children in this age group (see Chapter 6 for more information).

- They need the appropriate rules and regulations for all things digital (see Chapter 9 for more information).

- Try to not have your kids be too busy; instead connect with them daily—not teaching or lecturing but simply being with them. Allow them to be kids by not keeping them overly busy. Speak daily words of truth over them: "When you are a teenager, you are going to make great choices."

- If they haven't already, have them create for their bedrooms (and bathrooms) signs that say: "I am a son (or daughter) of God. Treat me lovingly."

- Teach them how to name their different feelings (especially boys) and teach them that our feelings are good and they tell us a lot about what's going on in our lives.

- Make sure you know the parents of their peers, which will be even more important as they move into the tween and teen years.

Start teaching children about bullying. In our opinion, some of the best information on bullying is from Barbara Coloroso. Check out her website at: www.kidsareworthit. com. She talks about the bully, the bullied, and the bystander and how to stop the insanity of bullying. It's an excellent resource.

Tween Years (10 - 12 years old)

Some of what 10-12 year olds need in our Catholic homes:

• They need the Word of God daily and they need us to pray with them daily (as a family), and they need to participate in weekly Mass with their family. They need to start giving back to their Church through time, talent, and treasure. (Many parishes have volunteer opportunities for young people in this age group and older.)

• Their bodies are already changing internally as puberty begins, so we need to teach them about healthy Christian sexuality (see Chapter 8 for more information).

• They need good Christian music to help them learn about God's love for them (Air One, or local Christian Radio). The old phrase "Garbage In, Garbage Out" (G.I.G.O.) can be turned into "Grace In, Grace Out." What we take in with our eyes and ears really does have an effect—for good or ill—on us.

• They need an active youth group or good Christian friends.

• They need us to be gentle with them and not raise our voices with them, because if we raise our voices frequently, this will raise their cortisol levels and over time it will work against us by potentially increasing the size of their amygdala in the brain (the fight, flight, or freeze center). Therefore, as parents, we must stay para-sympathetically dominant and use healthy tones and volumes.

• They need more age-related responsibilities and maybe a list of things they need to do daily (clean room, dust, start learning how to do laundry, help with food prep, etc.).

• Try to resist the cultural pull to let your kids become too busy. Instead, connect with them daily—not teaching or lecturing but simply "being with them." Make family time a priority. (Some families do this by limiting extra-curricular activities to one per child per season.) Keep speaking daily words of truth over them: "When you're a teenager, you're going to make great choices."

• At this age they can fill out the excellent inventory "The Five Love Languages for Children" (visit www.5lovelanguages.com).

• If they have cell phones or screens, they need to be monitored. We highly recommend Covenant Eyes (visit www.covenanteyes.com). You have a right, and even a responsibility, to review their texts and other online and social media interactions.

• Teach them (especially boys) how to name their different feelings and teach them that our feelings are good and they can tell us a lot about what is going on in our lives.

• Make sure you know the parents of your children's peers, and begin to pray about who will be their "go-to parents" when they are teens. These go-to parents should be active Christians and be trusted by your tween and you. When they become teens you can have a little meeting and explain to them the importance of these allies in the Body of Christ.

• Studies show that sharing four family meals per week pays great dividends in the teen years. Make this a priority now and it will help your family in the future.

• Try to take your tween on a fun retreat when they are 10. When they are 11, consider adding a purity curriculum on that retreat ("Passport to Purity," or other curriculum). Try to make that yearly retreat a consistent event in their lives. They will grow into it and look forward to it when they are teens.

• Watch for signs of depression, suicide, drug use, or other addiction issues, and get help ASAP from professionals if needed.

Teen Years (13-18 years old)

Some of what teens need in our Catholic homes:

In addition to the first six needs listed in the "tween" section, teens have particular requirements, based on their age and developing maturity:

• When they receive their driver's license, this is a great time to open up a checking account and continue to teach them the importance of giving back to the Church through time, talent, and treasure, as well as other Christian financial principles.

• Along with money management, teens need mentoring in time management. Help them maintain a reasonable balance in their schedule. High school and community sports are particularly challenging in this regard.

• We need to monitor all digital use carefully in the teen years. We highly recommend Covenant Eyes (www.covenanteyes.com). As with tweens, teens need a measure of oversight in their online and digital lives. Set limits on computer, TV, and cell phone usage. (More on this in Chapter 9.)

• We need to teach our teens (especially the guys) how to name their different feelings, that our feelings are good, and that they tell us a lot about what is going on in our lives.

• Teens naturally separate from their family of origin, so age 13 or 14 is the perfect age to select other go-to parents. These are parents whom both you and your teen trust. Take those parents and your teen (and their teen if they get along well and make good choices) out to coffee or have them over and explain to your child how much they are loved. Let them know that if they ever need to talk to any other parents about difficult issues, they can talk to these go-to parents. Then, close with a prayer and try to get together often with these go-to parents.

• Sharing just four meals a week as a family helps increase positive behaviors from our teens and decrease negative teen behaviors. Make this a priority.

• Teach all teens that they won't have an adult brain until they're about 24 years old. The "prefrontal cortex" (PFC) is not fully formed until age 24 or 25, and possibly later if there is chemical use. The PFC is used by the brain to override emotional impulses, which is one major reason why teens are so impulsive.

• Watch for signs of depression, suicide, drug use, or other addiction issues and get help ASAP from professionals if needed.

Our Children Need Prayer

Children need daily prayer time and time in the Word of God. The earlier we begin this habit, the better it will be received by our children. Of course, this time will wax and wane during family transitions: moving, birth of a baby, job stress, etc. But we still need to have a goal of sitting down every day to read the Bible and pray with our children. This will give them and us (as parents) a more secure foundation in our identity as children of God. If your children are older and they are not used to this habit, consider starting by listening to good Christian music and slowly integrating your faith life into your conversations with your children.

If working prayer time into your day seems difficult, consider this an invitation to examine how much time you spend in other pursuits (particularly screentime, i.e. TV, computer, Facebook, YouTube, etc.). If we are children of God and yet never set aside time to be with God, we are lacking a basic necessity in our lives. Just as our children need time with us as their parents, so do we all need time with our heavenly Father.

Before You Continue—Prayer

1) Do you spend daily prayer time together with your children most days?

If not, please take some time to identify the roadblocks that are preventing you from this critically important need for your family. Try to approach this exercise from a place of truth, not of shame.

2) The following are roadblocks to my goal of having more daily prayer time:

Now take a look at that list. Is there anything on that list that's more important than your relationship with the One who created you?

Again, this prayer time will wax and wane in the life of your family, and you need to have a balanced approach. If watching the nightly news is the reason you're not praying with your children, you can change that behavior. If, however, taking care of an ill mother or nursing your newborn is on that list, then that would be "lived prayer."

If you've never had consistent prayer time as a family and thinking about it tires you out because it's "one more thing to do," here's a model that we use.

We start with a reading from a Children's Bible (which we have changed and updated throughout the years). We talk about that reading and ask questions about it (try to stump the kids), and then we start to pray. Our prayer starts with spontaneous prayer for people, leaders, loved ones, etc. Then, one of us usually asks if there is anything anyone needs to apologize for that they hadn't already taken care of earlier . . . and we start! We forgive each other and close with an Our Father and other memorized prayers. Lately, our oldest daughter has asked us to include a time of silent prayer as well, which has been a wonderful addition; it is a sign that she claims this time as her own.

If you do have daily prayer time as a family but do not include Scripture, silent time, or some type of "ritual of forgiveness" time, perhaps now is a good time to add these and to see how God can use these in a powerful way to bless your family.

As your family grows to cherish this shared prayer time, you can expand it to include the Rosary, various devotions such as the Chaplet of Divine Mercy, the Jesus Prayer, the prayers of Mother Teresa and other recent saints, and in time you can introduce them to the Liturgy of the Hours, the Church's ancient daily morning and evening prayer.

Our Children Need Leadership

While prayer is essential, it's not the only thing our children need. They also need leadership in the home: either a strong marriage or a strong single parent. It seems to us a sad truth that in our nation we typically spend more money on our vehicles than we do on our marriages. And yet, it's the marriage that drives the family. Typically, as the marriage goes, so goes the family. For single parents this is even more difficult because you are the sole leader of your family.

If you're a single parent, first let us say that you are amazing! We admire the strength that single parents have and we pray for you. In the case of single parenting, children still need strong leadership from you. So please try to make sometime alone for your needs. If you need to talk to your parish about child care, please do so. Or, maybe you can talk to some of your friends from church about a babysitting co-op so that you can make more time for you.

For those of us who are married, it's essential that we make time to strengthen our marriages. This can be difficult in our busy lives. But the investment of time is not only crucial to the health of the marriage, it also brings benefits that last into the future. For all parents, time away is crucial. It may seem backwards, but taking time away from our children (and even our spouse) so that we can rejuvenate our spirits and rest our bodies makes it more possible for us to be present to them when we return. It is not selfish; it is life-giving for all of our relationships.

Before You Continue—Married Parents

1) What is the best time of day for the two of you to connect?

2) When was your last "date" as a couple? How important is it to you to have regular dates?

3) When do the two of you get away together? Does each of you manage to schedule retreat time occasionally? What makes this possible? What hinders it?

Before You Continue—Single Parents

Who makes up your support system so that you can get some time away? How can you schedule more of this time if you currently aren't doing so?

Our Children Need Validation

Our children need positive attitudes and actions from us, including the power of validation. Not everyone is good at validating; it depends on family of origin, personality, how tired someone is, etc. Many in our "instant fix" society have difficulties validating their children. When we validate a child we show them that we know what they are saying from an emotional point of view. Paul says it best in Rom. 12:15: "Be happy with those who are happy, and be sad with those who are sad." What a powerful scriptural challenge it is to validate!

For example, if your child comes to you with a school problem and tells you that a classmate called her stupid, you might be inclined to immediately "fix" it by telling her that she is not stupid. Yet that is not a validating statement, and it sometimes only acts to cover up a hurt that a child needs to talk about and resolve. In this case, a validating action would be for you to get down to her level, look her in eyes, and say "I am sorry that happened; do you want to talk more about that?" This is a challenge when we have other kids to care for, supper to make, bills to pay, calls to make, and messes to clean up.

Yet, if we consistently and effectively validate our children, they will continue to open up to us, trust us with future topics, and really feel heard so that they know they can talk to us about any topic on their minds or in their hearts. When we validate, especially early on in our children's lives, we are laying a foundation for trust and security, and we are increasing the odds that our children will want to continue to share their difficulties with us because they will feel heard.

Before we move deeper into validation, let's talk about the need to "fix" things. We certainly agree that we need to "fix" things at times. For example, in the above example you would eventually come to the truth with your child that she is not stupid. The problem is that we tend to try to fix things before we validate. For building trust in a relationship with our children, validation before fixing is essential.

Take a moment now to think about the Validation Scale below. On a scale of 1-10, circle how well you think you validate your children and your loved ones. (A "10" is the highest and is rare.) After you have circled the number you think best fits you, have your spouse or a loved one (it could even be your child) circle a number that they think describes you. Then compare your answers. Talk about any discrepancies. While you're talking about this with your loved one, listen, validate, and learn; don't defend.

Validation Scale

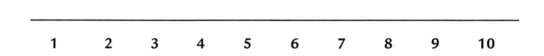

If your number is lower than 8, we invite you to work on this skill of validating.

Some Validating Basics

If you hear "bad" news from a child, say, "I'm sorry to hear that; do you want to talk more about that?" If you hear "good" news from the child, you can say with a smile: "That's great; would you like to talk more about that?"

A point of clarification is in order here: using the word "sorry" as in the above example doesn't mean that you are taking the blame or the responsibility for it. That is certainly one meaning of the word but not the one intended here. Rather, "sorry" means, "As a fellow human being who is sad when people suffer, I am sorry for the pain you're experiencing now."

Our Children Need Play

Our children also need for us to play with them and enter into their world. This can be another challenge, especially if we don't value play or recreational time. We have become so production-oriented in our society to feed the economy that we have forgotten the importance of play and Sabbath. When we take time to enter into our children's world it is a "lived validation." Our children will appreciate it and they will feel that close bond that Christ desires in our family.

If your child is into video games we encourage you to try some out, expand your horizons, and have a little fun. But recognize that not all video games are created equal. There are plenty of games out there that are not only completely contrary to Gospel values but are so real they blur the line between reality and fiction for our children. These games don't belong in our homes because of their sexual content and violent messages. Again, we are called to be domestic churches, and these types of games do not encourage our children in their identity as children of God.

If your children are younger, play with them, have fun, use your imagination, and even use play time for learning. Jim has played dolls with our girls and has been the little boy named "Alex." Alex was a smart little boy, and part of their play time was about Alex going to school and learning his multiplication tables. The girls still talk about Daddy being Alex at times, and this has become a wonderful memory in our family.

Our Children Need Physical Activity and Exercise

Another discipline most children need is regular physical activity. If this is a need for your children, we suggest re-reading the section on how Christ left us the example of exercise and how we need to follow His lead (see pages 26-27). We need to help our children identify what activities they like to do and then encourage them and even reward them for doing those activities. This can instill in our children a love for physical activity.

There are so many wonderful activities that we can do together: walking, biking, rollerblading, swimming, martial arts, and more.

Our Children Need Sleep

Our children also need regular sleep patterns. We're amazed at how sleep-deprived we as a culture have let our children become, and we're convinced that some (if not many) of the emotional and behavioral problems we see with our children are partly due to lack of sleep. Sleep is the body's built-in mechanism for renewal and restoration. Let's take a look at sleep needs in children, according to the National Sleep Foundation.

Newborns will sleep about 10.5 to 18 hours a day depending on the baby. One of the best books we have found regarding newborn sleep patterns is *On Becoming Baby Wise* by Gary Ezzo and Robert Bucknam, M.D. Like most books there are points to disagree with, but overall for sleep patterns of newborns this is a helpful resource.

Toddlers (1-3 years old) need about 12-14 hours of sleep every day. Of course most toddlers also nap, although some phase that out (our second daughter did . . . that was hard). Build your toddler's schedule around rituals of waking, eating, playing, napping and sleeping (for 12-14 hours) and see how the Lord can work in your family life.

Preschoolers (3-5 years old) need about 11-13 hours of sleep everyday but usually don't nap after about the age of five. These are busy years and parents need to be vigilant about their own needs as they navigate these stages.

School aged children (5-12 years old) need 10-11 hours of sleep every day, and this is in the midst of ever-increasing social and academic engagements. Here is where parents' use of leverages can really pay off (see Chapter 6 for more information). Telling our children that they can choose only one extracurricular activity per season or enforcing other types of limitations can build in more sleeping time.

Teens need around 8.5 to 9.5 hours of sleep every night, and adults need about 7 to 8 hours every night. It is during these teen years that many teens (though not all) tend to push their parents and family aside in order to have more time with peers. Even though this happens, parents are still very important to teens, and we need to make sure that our teens are getting enough sleep via curfews, boundaries, and consistent consequences (see Chapter 5 for more information).

Before You Continue—Sleep Needs

After reading the guidelines from the National Sleep Foundation, ask yourself: How are you and your children meeting your needs for sleep?

Tips That Have Helped Other Parents

Before bedtime, use rituals incorporating prayer, quiet time and absolutely NO TV or screentime for at least a few hours before bed. If your child relies on screens to get to sleep, try slowly easing off that habit. Give yourself a reasonable timeframe (about a month or two). Then set up a reward system and a gradual slowing, and eventual stopping, of the TV watching.

For example, if your child watches two hours of TV before going to bed, you'll want to change that. For the first week, reduce it to one hour and 45 minutes and then have a small reward for every night that goal is met (it might be stickers for younger children; it might be cash, cell phone privileges, extra trips, etc. for tweens or teens). The next week go down to an hour and a half, then an hour the next week, etc. When the goal is reached every day and every week make sure you reward that with your pre-determined reward. This will reinforce the new habit you are trying to teach.

A similar plan could work for getting a child to sleep earlier, as well. If your child is getting to sleep at 9 p.m. and needs to be sleeping at 8 p.m., slowly and consistently have the child go to sleep earlier each week, working in 15-minute increments each week. By week four you will have met your goal. Again, use consistent rewards to ensure that the child will continue this habit.

Our Children Need Time

Do you know how children spell the word "love?" They spell it T-I-M-E; they always have and always will. We need to spend good quality time with our children. In order to facilitate that, our children need good temporal boundaries. Many parents keep children so busy, perhaps trying to vicariously live out things they couldn't do (sports, arts, etc.) in their own youth. Some children have busier schedules than their parents do. Not only does this take away precious family time (think of the word "love"), but it also creates hectic schedules that gradually increase anxieties and blood pressure and wreak havoc on relationships.

Discuss with your spouse, (or a loved one if you're a single parent) what realistic limits are, and then present them to your child in the form of choices: (e.g., "Do you want to play soccer or piano?") We tend to give our children too many choices, overloading them and keeping them in a constant state of stimulation. Include in your schedule some quiet time where you can all be still and let God love you.

Before You Continue—Our Children's Needs

1) What was most the helpful information for you in this chapter?

2) How will that information help transform your parenting?

3) What needs to change in your own life in order for you to help meet the needs of your children?

Prayer About Our Children's Needs

All good and giving God, You are the great provider and we thank You. Thinking about all of our children's needs can be overwhelming. Please send me Your Spirit to calm my worries, and help me to trust in Your loving care. Continue to provide for my needs so that I can provide for the needs of my children. I ask this through Christ our Lord and in the power of the Holy Spirit. Amen.

5

Fifth Daily Dozen:
Learn and Use Good Communication Skills

"In the beginning was the Word, and the Word was with God and the Word was God." —John 1:1

It's amazing that God has placed a priority on communicating His love to us. Have you ever thought about that? Jesus the Christ, the Second Person of the Blessed Trinity, is the eternal "Word" of God, and God chose to communicate that Love to us. In other words, when we communicate in a healthy way, it's a lived prayer because we are imitating Abba, who constantly communicates love to His people. It's essential in our parenting to examine the priority that we place on communication with our loved ones.

Jim remembers the distress of one client who reported she had a good pre-teen child but that it was hard to get him to talk to her any more. Jim asked what her son liked and she replied, "Football." That was a helpful response, because Jim knew they had some good potential for connecting.

Jim told this mom that she needed to talk to her son in a language he would understand. He recommended that she use some football terms. "What do you mean?" was her response. "Ask your son what happens if the team does not communicate well," he suggested to her. She did that, and her son immediately opened up, because he understood that their family is much like a team that needs to work together. This story summarizes the importance of this Daily Dozen: we need to address our children in a language they will understand without neutralizing the importance of our message. Sports (and other topics) work well for this. If your child doesn't like team sports, work with examples that they do like: it might be hunting, math, arts, music, etc. It may take some creativity, but with prayer and guidance, you can find a language and examples from their life that can speak to them about the importance of working together as a team and the need for order.

Before You Continue—Our Children's Activities

1) What's important to your children? What are some activities they love to do?

2) How can you relate these activities to the need for good communication with your children?

Tones and Volumes

Healthy communication is challenging. It's sometimes too easy to yell at our children to get them to do something. There are several problems with this. First, as parents we are modelling for our children what they should do. Second, and probably more important, if we raise our voices too often even to a newborn, this raises cortisol levels in the baby's body. Cortisol is a stress hormone, and while it's very important, the body needs balance. When cortisol is out of balance through too much yelling—or other external or internal stress—it can actually alter the child's brain chemistry and lead to more aggressive behavior. So when we yell as parents, we're literally working against ourselves because it will lead to more defiant behavior from our children.

Instead of yelling, we recommend using correct and consistent leverages, which we'll cover in the next chapter. Tones and volumes are crucial in our communication patterns with our children. If our tones are sarcastic or disrespectful and our volumes are loud, do we really expect our children to listen to and obey us? Many of us don't know the literal meaning of the word sarcasm. Do you know what it means? The word is from the Greek root "sarx," and "sarcasm" literally means "to tear the flesh off." When we think about what sarcasm means, it seems best to avoid it.

Before You Continue—Tones and Volumes

1) Take a moment to pray and think about the tones and volumes you use with your children and loved ones. Are they healthy? Are they effective in communicating your love to them?

2) Do you repeat some tones and volumes that you learned as a child? If so, did you like those as a child? Do you really want to repeat them?

3) Do your tones and volumes need to change? If so, what is one thing you can do today to begin that change? See below for a list of suggestions that parents can use.

If you need to work on tones and volumes, as most of us do at times, it might help to resolve to count to 10 before you use a negative tone or volume with your child or loved one. And it might be helpful to share this with a trusted friend so you can work on figuring out why you're using those tones and volumes. For example, you might be tired of repeating yourself, or you might be just plain tired. You might need to re-read the section on who you are and what you need, because if you're communicating in ways you don't want to, perhaps your needs aren't being met. It's good to know the reason we're using certain tones and volumes with our children.

Other helpful suggestions include that reminder on the bathroom mirror that we are all members of the Body of Christ, and we share in Christ's identity. Jesus told us that what we do to the least of our brothers and sisters we do to Him. On a good day, this helps us realize that when we talk to our children, we're talking to Christ. In addition, you can also use leverages (so you don't have to repeat yourself), along with taking care of some of your needs; these all help you to be aware of your unhealthy tones.

And when you make a mistake, try to ask for forgiveness.

If you have a hard time with yelling (which is true for most parents we have worked with), first, be gentle with yourself. Try using these seven strategies daily before a conflict or "storm." They will help you prepare the soil, plant the seeds, weed, and tend to the "relationship garden."

A Proven Method You Can Use Now to Step Yelling

1) Pray the "Don't Yell" prayer several times a day, and associate being angry or frustrated with deep breathing and saying this prayer:

> *"Jesus, with Your peace, I don't need to yell.*
> *I can take a deep breath and be calm."*

This prayer calms your soul and mind, and the deep breaths calm your body and allow the neocortex portion of your brain to think first and not act out of anger or frustration. Do this several times a day; it will help because you'll be creating an intellectual and spiritual expectation of what will actually happen when you're angry or frustrated. We highly recommend that you put this formula in your smartphone or a daily calendar, or wherever you'll see it often.

Think about this in terms of planting a garden of good communication between you and your children. In order to have a good garden you need to do certain behaviors before, during, and after a storm. We need to cultivate the soil, fertilize it, and protect it from frost and storms. The "storms" in our analogy are the times when we yell or experience a lot of stress in our relationship.

2) Understand and use the gift of prayerful imagination. Imagine getting angry or frustrated and not yelling! Imagination is very powerful, and this technique has been used for decades by professional athletes and others to improve their skills. It works because the brain has a hard time differentiating between imagination and reality. So, if you devote time to imagine getting frustrated with your children by using all five of your senses, and then imagine praying your "Don't Yell" prayer, taking a deep breath, and not yelling, you're setting up your brain to do just that when it happens in reality. Try it; it works!

3) Think and pray daily on Matthew 25:40. "What you do to the least of my brothers and sisters you do to me." When I choose to yell at my children, I am literally yelling at Christ. This alone changed the behaviors of one dad Jim worked with. Because his dad was not yelling as much, his son offered him more hugs.

4) Slow down: expectations, driving, talking, and moving. Then, re-invest in your relationship with your children. Don't try to cram too much in a day—especially during the weekend. Slowing down can help us be more patient with ourselves and with our children. Instead of staying too busy, devote at least 15 minutes a day to just being with your children—without screens. This bonding is one of the best ways to prevent "storms" that can threaten the garden of our relationship with our children.

5) Know each other's pet peeves and anger triggers and discuss ways to minimize them by saying "No, please." Understand the triggers that your kids do that increase your anger and lead to yelling. Discuss minimizing the triggers by saying "No, please" and continue to work on responding in a different way when anger triggers get activated.

6) Make sure your top needs are being met. In working with hundreds of parents over the years in various settings, both of us can attest that when primary needs are being met, parents tend to yell less because they're less stressed. Get those needs met. (see Chapter 3 for tips.)

7) Cultivate silence and create quiet spaces; turn off the background noise. Devote at least six minutes to meditation every day, which is all it takes to start positively changing your brain chemistry. Start slowly and build to six minutes.

A Step-by-Step Guide to Christian Meditation You Can Start Today

• **First, you'll need a quiet spot and a slower pace**; those tasks by themselves aren't easy. If you're new to Christian meditation, it may be helpful to have a clock so you can keep track of the time. Some like to set the alarm for three minutes or so, but others find this too jarring and would rather just keep an eye on the time.

Try starting slowly . . . meditate a few minutes at a time and see how it goes. As for the quiet space that's needed, you can choose a church or a quiet spot in the house after the kids go to bed (instead of watching TV or surfing the net). You can also try a quiet place at work, if you're blessed to have one.

• **Second, select a word or phrase from the Scriptures** that speaks peace into your life. Some choose "peace," "I am precious," or "I am loved." You can meditate on the name "Jesus" because "at the name of Jesus every knee should bend . . . " (Philippians 2:10). That includes the very strong "knees" of your anxiety; it has no choice but to humbly bow as you meditate on the Holy Name.

• **Third, once you're in your quiet space and you've chosen your word or phrase, get into a comfortable position**, but not so comfy that you fall asleep (meditation is not hibernation). Once you're comfortable, start to say your word or phrase softly to yourself, or even gently audibly, if that helps and you're alone.

Say it slowly and let your word or phrase sink deeply within you, permeating all you are. Once you slow down to this pace, your mind will flood with thoughts, worries, concerns of the day or year, and memories. It seems that in our brokenness we have a very hard time being still and knowing that God is God. Don't worry about that normal response. The good news is that the more you meditate, the quieter your mind and thought processes can become. There are some points to remember when you start slowing down and the thoughts burst in. Adopt a semi-passive attitude toward those incoming thoughts and continue to repeat your focus word or phrase.

Also, recognize that for all practical purposes, most incoming thoughts fit into two categories: 1) "neutral" thoughts (bills to pay, stress during the day, kids to feed, taking the dog to the vet, etc.), and 2) temptation.

The "neutral thoughts" are normal thoughts that threaten to distract us. The second category is temptations (temptations to think something uncharitable, to say something unkind, to judge someone unjustly, etc.). Now, let's talk about applying a semi-passive attitude to the two categories of thoughts that can be present when we slow down. For the first category, the "neutral" thoughts, it's important not to fight them. Instead, a semi-passive attitude recognizes they are there and then immediately goes back to repeating the focus word or phrase. We call it a "semi-passive" attitude, because if the thought is a blatant temptation, the second category of thoughts, it's good to simply rebuke that temptation by saying "No" to it, and then going back to the word or phrase.

An example may help illustrate. Jim recalls meditating in front of the Blessed Sacrament in a local church. When he started to repeat his word or phrase ("Jesus") he was distracted by a neutral thought (probably something about work), so he simply recognized the thought and then went back to meditating. He said something like, "Yep, I know you're here, but I'm thinking about Jesus right now." That helped him calm down and focus more on his point of meditation (the powerful name of Jesus). During that same meditation time he was tempted to think an uncharitable thought. He responded to the temptation with a sharp rebuke: "No. I'm meditating on the name of Jesus." The rebuke helped him to stay focused on his meditation phrase. The more meditation we have our in life, the easier this process becomes.

Strategies to Use During a Conflict

The following are strategies to use during a conflict with your children. Using the garden metaphor, this would be what you do during a frost or a storm. If you don't take immediate action, your gardens will be harmed and much of the hard work you have invested (cultivating, planting, pulling weeds, etc.) can be lost. These steps protect the relationship from any storms. They should be used as soon as possible during a conflict.

Steps to Take During a Conflict

1) Use the "Don't Yell" prayer and take deep breaths frequently. Don't think that because this is so simple it's not effective. That couldn't be further from the truth. Saying the "Don't Yell" prayer will help calm the mind and the soul, and taking deep breaths from the diaphragm can ensure there is adequate blood flow to the prefrontal cortex, thereby helping us not to act on the anger or frustrations we're feeling. Breathe in God's love and breathe out the toxic feelings.

2) Stay para-sympathetically dominant. Muscle relaxation, deep breathing, and staying in the present moment are all strategies to help your body stay relaxed (i.e. in the parasympathetic zone and not stressed by being too sympathetically dominant). This is hard to do, but it's so necessary during a conflict. It helps protect the relationship and enables us as parents to think clearly.

3) Stay out of the chaos. When our kids have meltdowns we need to stay out of the chaos so that we don't add to it. If we enter into the chaos, we've already increased the storm. By staying outside of the meltdown and chaos we have an opportunity to model for our children what's appropriate to do when we're feeling angry or frustrated (i.e., staying calm). We don't need to act on these powerful feelings generated by the amygdala; instead, we can rely on the prefrontal cortex and model a calm, peaceful response.

4) Remember that your child is being a child. Our children won't have a fully formed prefrontal cortex until they're about 24 or 25 years old. Because of their culture, our kids are mostly sympathetically dominant, due to too much stimulation, not enough sleep, not enough exercise, poor diet, and poor parenting. Since they let go of their social expectations when they're feeling safe (like when they're at home), we need to be patient and give them some room to work through hard feelings.

5) Initiate a time out for both parties by making the "T" symbol with your hands. After making the "T" symbol, say something like, "I love you so much I don't want to argue with you, so let's both take a timeout for 10 minutes and calm down and talk about this at _____ (time)." Then follow through with good communication techniques.

Strategies to Use After a Conflict

Again, using the garden metaphor, this is when we cooperate with the Holy Spirit and allow grace to turn our waste products (hurts, raised voices, etc.) into fertilizer to continue to feed the garden of our relationship. This can only be done by the power of the Holy Spirit (Rom. 8:28).

1) Decide to forgive and reconcile. Talk about the disagreement together. Review the forgiveness fundamentals if you need to (these are found in Chapter 7, "We are the Parents.") This is a critical step to making sure the Lord heals and resurrects these hurts.

2) Learn from it in order to not repeat it. As in any relationship, we need to own our mistakes and we need to encourage children to own their mistakes—not with shame but with truth. The truth reminds us we are children of God and we learn from our mistakes.

3) Don't be defeated when it happens again. Just work the plan and the plan will work. We're human, and the Lord knows that. When disagreements happen, continue to follow this simple yet effective plan to create a beautiful life-giving garden of good communication between you and your children. If major problems continue and you're having a difficult time executing these steps, it's time to talk to a pastor or a Christian therapist for some healing work. Not with shame but with a sense of hope, we recognize that we all need help with some things in our lives. There's no shame in asking for help, because God wants to heal and help you grow an awesome garden of communication with your children.

The Importance of Non-Verbals

Of course, communication is more than just tones and volumes. Communication is also about non-verbals, or what is not said. How are your non-verbal skills?

There are four powerful actions that we can do from the neck up that speak louder than any words can. Do you know what those four non-verbal actions are? Think about the acronym "S-E-E-N." Take time to write out below what you think these critical four actions are. Talk about them. The answers are on page 131.

S _____

E _____

E _____

N_____

Have you practiced any of these four yet? If not, please don't wait. These non-verbals are potent in showing our children that we care for them and we love them; they're a healing salve to any unhealthy tones and volumes we sometimes use.

What is Heard is More Important Than What is Said

Another difficult reality of communication is that not only is communication about what wasn't said (the non-verbals), it's also about what is heard by the receiver of the message. You can say something and what the other person heard is not at all what you intended. Has that ever happened to you? It's very frustrating and can automatically set the conversation on several negative courses.

To avoid this common pitfall in communication, you and your child can start practicing the phrase "What I heard was . . ." and then they repeat what they heard you say. This gives you a chance to clarify if that is what you really meant. Use this phrase and teach it to your children so that you can begin to correct any misunderstanding.

Another good way to teach our children to harness their anger is to talk about our "anger and stress bottle." Stress and anger can generate and aggravate one other. When life is stressful we can become angry, and when we become angry we get stressed out. Anger is a common human emotion and is not the problem. The problem is what we do with our anger. If we think about containing it in our internal "anger and stress bottle," we can start to harness it.

Suggest to your children that when they're angry or stressed, they tell those feelings "I know I'm feeling (angry or stressed) but I'm not going to act on them right now." Instead, put them in your "bottle" and tell the feelings "I will let you out later." Later should ideally be that same day. When you're exercising and start sweating, open up your bottle and let the feelings out! This can be an effective way to harness your stress and anger so it doesn't harness you.

More Good Parental Communication Tips

1) Know each other's "pet peeves." Everyone is entitled to their own odd habits, and in a family it is important that we talk about them openly instead of letting those human quirks drive us nuts. For example, one of Maureen's pet peeves is the sound that crinkling cellophane makes (think of a potato chip bag). There's no logic to it: it's just intensely annoying to her. And each member of our family seems to have his or her own irritant. We've learned each other's pet peeves so that we can try to avoid them. We don't get it perfect, and when we make mistakes we ask for forgiveness and try not to do it again. This helps our family act like more of a team. Why would you ever do something that you know a loved one hates? It makes no sense whatsoever. The phrase we use if someone is doing a pet peeve is "No, please." That's it, and that helps our family tremendously.

2) Avoid absolutes such as "always" and "never" in conversations; they seldom lead to good patterns of dialogue. Instead use words like "most of the time," or "rarely."

3) Try not to carry on difficult conversations after 8 or 9 p.m. Our wills and intellect need to be fresh when we discuss difficult topics. There's a reason why brainwashing is associated with sleep deprivation. Our wills and intellect are among the first faculties to fade as we become tired. If there's anger present, it might be best to first create some time to "cool off" before trying to communicate. This isn't giving up, nor is it being a weak parent. Quite the contrary; it's being a wise parent. When humans become angry it can change our thought patterns, and sometimes we need to allow our children (or ourselves) to productively work out their anger before we can communicate. There are many good ways to work out anger. Have children draw their anger out to show them they can harness it. Maybe have them write it out and then safely burn it with you (our kids love this ritual). Relaxation techniques or counting to 10 can be helpful. Listen to soothing music or perhaps think about the anger and exercise it out.

Before You Continue

1) Do you know each other's pet peeves? What are they?

2) Do you try to respect them and avoid them in front of each other?

3) What method will work best for your family to address the stress that can come from pet peeves?

Prayer About Communication

All good and ever present God, You give us the great gift of communication in order to imitate You. Send Your Word into our hearts so that we can use our tongues in ways that will build Your Kingdom in our family. Anoint our words so that we can effectively communicate Your love to one another in word and deed. We pray this through Christ our Lord and in the power of Your Holy Spirit. Amen.

Sixth Daily Dozen: Thanks be to God for Leverages! **6**

". . . be wise as serpents and innocent as doves." —Matthew 10:16

Leverages are tools in family life that you're probably already using. Our prayer is that if you're using them this chapter will help you refine them. If you've never used leverages as a discipline tool, welcome to the wonderful world of parental manipulation (in the best sense of the term). This chapter is all about correct and consistent consequences, leverages, and disciplining your children. We like using leverages because it imitates what Abba does with us; everyday, we as adults have choices and we need to learn how to make good choices. Leverages teach our children to make good choices, too.

Most of these techniques work well for most children. However, in the case of some childhood disorders (ADHD, autism, abuse, etc.), it's best to seek out professional help before implementing them. While these leverages, and this workbook, can work with children who have mental health diagnoses, it's always best to seek out professional help first and perhaps use these ideas along with therapy.

God has given parents all the earthly power in their families. This is a great responsibility, and we need to make sure that we are wise stewards of that power by making time for prayer. Our families are not democracies; instead they are more like a benevolent dictatorship (more about this later). Of course we want to seek input from our children and validate and listen to that input. But fundamentally, we are in control and we need to allow the Spirit to work in our decisions. Leverages help us exercise our parental power so we don't need to repeat ourselves, nag our children, or misuse our power.

What is a leverage? Simply defined, a "leverage" is an easier way to move something. If you are trying to move a piano, the smartest strategy is to get help and use a leveraged machine such as a two wheeled device to pick it up and move it. In a family, if you are trying to "move" a toddler or a teen (or any stage in-between), the best way to proceed is to get help (this workbook, other friends, pastors, etc.) and use a leveraged machine (your words and their privileges, along with correct and consistent discipline).

Leverages are not needs, but rather wants and privileges that you let your children do. What we're trying to move are the attitudes and actions of our children. We think leverages work best for that job.

How Do I Know and Use My Child's Leverages?

First, understand who your children are as children of God and understand your identity as well. Pray and think about what your children love to do and privileges that you allow them to do; both are potential leverages. Some examples could be playing on the computer, watching TV, using their cell phones, using the Internet, etc. (Don't make the same mistake as one dad, who used youth group time as a leverage.) Leverages are wants—not needs; they are privileges. Every child has wants. If you aren't sure what your child loves to do, or wants to do, watch him or her for a day or two and take notes. We advise not using sweets or other foods as leverages so as to not create negative dynamics with food; it's best to use other wants or likes in your child's life. Parents should compile this list as a couple.

Write Down Your Child's Leverages and Prioritize Them

Write down and prioritize the top three or four things each of your children like to do. If you have five children, you'll have five separate lists. Because leverages are about wants and not needs, we advise against including time with Christian friends, good relatives, etc. as a leverage because children need those relationships.

The reason you want to prioritize this list is that, if possible, you never want to get close to their favorite (#1) privilege. Always start with number three of four. If you need to use the number one leverage, split it up by dividing that activity into a quantity of time they spend doing that specific activity. This applies to the other leverages as well, so instead of an "all or nothing mentality" the leverages can be split up into half-hour or hour segments.

The Family Meeting

Now that you have your list of the prioritized leverages, hold a family meeting and begin with a prayer. In the meeting discuss how much you love your children and how you want to include a new (or revised) way of running the house. Let them know that in the future if they display any attitudes or actions that are not appropriate, they will be warned once. If they choose to continue the attitude or action they will lose a privilege (leverage). Be specific about the attitudes and actions you are talking about: tones, volumes, not listening to mom or dad the first time, too much sibling fighting (some is normal and actually teaches good lessons), disrespecting each other's boundaries, etc. Some families find it helpful to write down these rules. It's a very helpful step, but leverages can work with or without writing rules down. You'll increase your child's compliance if you write down what behavior you're trying to change, such as tones and disrespect.

Never Take Anything Away!

During the initial meeting, allow your children to review their own leverages. If you want to receive their input for their leverages that's OK, but remember that ultimately it's up to you as the parent. One of the keys of leveraging is to never take privileges away, because it's about the child making choices. Not only does this teach our children the indispensable lesson of consequences, but it also means they can never blame us, even though they'll try. Ultimately, they are in control over which privileges they will have or not have. So this phrase will never be used, "If you continue that action I will take your TV time away." Instead we tell our children, without emotion, "If you continue that action, you are choosing to lose half an hour (or more) of your TV time today. You choose; this is your one warning."

Take Emotions Out of It . . . Don't Join the Chaos

Another key of leveraging is for you as the parent to not use emotion when you give the warning and when you let them know that they are choosing to lose a privilege. Bringing emotion into the situation only complicates it for you and your child. Instead, say in a factual way, "This is your one warning; if you choose to continue to do (whatever they are doing) you are choosing to lose (whatever the privilege is)." This can be difficult, and you may need to re-read some of what you need in order to take emotion out of the equation.

Possible Earn-Back

Sometimes you can allow children to earn their leverages back, but if you do, make it random so that your child doesn't manipulate you. If you allow them to earn the privilege back, you can come up with a list of activities that need to be done before the privilege is earned back, such as cleaning the toilet, washing the dishes, or cleaning their room.

Real Clinical Example of Leverages

Jim worked with a family of a teen and they wanted to try the leverages; they thought it was a great idea. They discovered their teen's leverages (what the teen wanted) and they prioritized their list: 1) Car privilege, 2) Internet, and 3) Cell phone use. So, when their teen used a disrespectful tone or action towards his parents or siblings, the parents issued a warning without emotion. If it happened again then he decided to lose his cell phone for 30 minutes (or longer). If another offense came up, a non-emotional warning was issued and if it was not heeded then he decided to lose 30 minutes (or more) of his Internet privilege that day. If another offense came up another non-emotional warning would be issued, and if that offense was repeated he would choose to lose 30 minutes (or more) of car privilege. These leverages, along with other changes in family dynamics, have helped this family heal.

What About Really Abusive Behavior?

Although it doesn't happen in every family, there are times when teens will try to fight back physically because they don't like their parents using leverages. If a teen ever lays a hand on a parent, or seriously threatens to, we always recommend calling the police. That can usually wake the kid up to the fact that you will not bend on this issue and that they cannot hurt Mom or Dad. We hope and pray this never happens in your family, but if it does, God can bring good from it. God loves us with a powerful love. There's nothing complicated about this type of discipline, but it does take consistent and correct application of the leverages. This does work, but you may notice that your children's attitudes and actions will get a bit worse before they get better. This can be very normal. Please stay consistent and use leverages correctly so they can help. Again, it takes about 60 days for a new habit to be internalized for adults; your children need time as well.

Before You Continue

1) Are you using leverages in your parenting?

2) Do you know the prioritized leverages you would use for each of your children? If so, are they written down?

3) Do you want your child to earn back privileges?

Reduce Leverages by "Catching" Them Doing the Good

Another discipline tip that needs some press time is not about leveraging but is based on the axiom that love is always willing to "catch" the other person doing the good, and will consequently reward that person for the good, either verbally or physically. If we as parents tried harder to follow that axiom of parenting, we would probably use leverages much less often.

Jim remembers working with a family and using one of the clinic's play-therapy rooms (two rooms connected with a two-way mirror for observation purposes). He was meeting with the Mom and Dad in the observation room while the children were playing in the playroom. In the middle of the session Jim excused himself and walked out of the observation room and knocked on the door of the children's room.

Their little faces looked shocked as he walked in their room. An adult coming into their space while they were playing could only mean one thing: they were doing something wrong or being too loud or something needed correcting. Upon entering the playroom he knelt down and told them, "I am proud of you! You are doing a great job of playing in here; keep up the wonderful work!" When he left, their faces were beaming with self-love and self-confidence. They continued that behavior for the rest of their session. The parents loved that and learned from it. Unfortunately, we don't always build upon the good actions and attitudes of our children, but rewarding the good remains the best behavior modification. "Sticker charts" or charts that kids make up to earn items for good behavior are essential in parenting.

Give Your Children a Heads-Up

Another great tip when it comes to disciplining is to always let your children know what is coming up next. With younger children this can be difficult because they might not be able to tell time. But a buzzer set for five minutes and a statement that tells them "when the buzzer goes off, we're going to get our pajamas on, brush our teeth, and say prayers" is much more effective than springing these commands on them without notice.

Before You Continue

1) Recall a recent instance of your child doing good. Did you tell him or her you were pleased with that behavior?

2) What is one thing you will do differently as a parent, based on this chapter?

Prayer About Leverages

Ever gracious God, Your Son told us to be as gentle as doves and as cunning as serpents. Send Your Holy Spirit into my heart today so that I may continue to discipline my children in smarter ways and not harder ways. Help me to work with Your wisdom to form my children into Your image and likeness. I ask this through Christ our Lord and in the power of the Holy Spirit. Amen.

7

Seventh Daily Dozen: We Are the Parents!

"Children, obey your parents in the Lord, for this is right." —Ephesians 6:1

We were both blessed to spend time during school studying abroad. Our time in the Middle East gave us a particular appreciation for the freedoms we routinely enjoy in this country: no security checkpoints, the ability to gather freely and to go where we want, etc. The degree of freedom we enjoy in this country is a blessing not to be taken for granted.

We see this abuse of freedom frequently while shopping: kids debating with their parents about buying something. If Mom or Dad say "No" (a word children need to hear) it's common for children to debate because they think the family is a democracy, and they think they have equal power. But families are not democratic.

God has given parents earthly authority, and God desires that parents use this to help children become more of who they truly are: children of God! While discussion has its place, we need to end debates and let our "Yes mean Yes" and our "No mean No."

God has set up families with order and structure, and our children depend on that order. God calls parents to be stewards of these precious children. This chapter focuses on concrete ways we can become better stewards of our families.

Types of Parenting

Understanding what type of parent you are is critical in becoming a better steward and leader.

Over the years theorists have developed a "parenting quadrant" that serves as a helpful guide to understanding what type of parenting we do. It's comprised of two major necessities in a family: 1) Rules and 2) Warmth (sometimes called "positive regard").

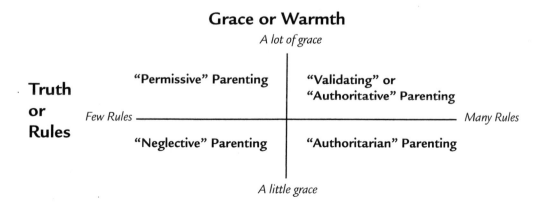

We call these two "truth and grace" from the Gospel of John (1:14). Jesus is "full of grace and truth" perfectly. We don't get it perfect, so there's a continuum instead. "Truth" is the rules we use or the structure we use. "Grace" is the warmth in our house and the validation that we offer. These both exist on a grid from low to high, as seen in the diagram above.

The upper left quadrant is called "Permissive" because there is high "grace" (or a lot of "warmth") and only a few rules, which leads to a permissive parenting style. In this type of family there aren't enough boundaries for the children. It would serve the parents well to create more boundaries and rules. We recommend these parents read *Boundaries with Children* by Dr. Henry Cloud and Dr. John Townsend.

The upper right quadrant is called "Validating," or "Authoritative" (which is a good word). This is the best style of parenting, representing parents who have many rules and a lot of grace. Many rules mean predictability and even some flexibility. Good rules are clearly established by either writing them down or discussing them in a healthy manner. Also, you'll notice that the warmth (or grace) is high, meaning that parents emotionally validate their children, as we discussed in Chapter 4.

The lower left quadrant is called the "Neglectful" parenting style because there are few rules and not much warmth or grace. Another term for this type of parenting is chaotic. The children run the show and don't receive much love or validation. The children need healthy adults in their lives who will love them enough to both validate them and set limits for them.

The lower right quadrant is called "Authoritarian" because these parents have many rules (high truth) but there's not much grace or warmth in the family. With this type of parenting the children will frequently hear about following the rules (usually with unhealthy tones and volumes), but they'll rarely feel loved by the parent because there is not much validating going on. This is very sad for the children, and it can feel like a heavy-handed household, not at all what Christ has planned for His children.

Before You Continue—Parenting Styles

1) Take a look at the graphic again and talk to your loved ones about these parenting styles. What type of parenting are you using?

2) Are you pleased with that type?

3) Consider that the validating/authoritative parenting style is most effective. How can you move toward this type of parenting?

Family of Origin

A chapter on how we are the parents wouldn't be complete without discussing where we first learned about being parents—i.e., our family of origin. It's critical to evaluate what type of parenting your parents taught, as well as other issues in your family of origin. It's also imperative to know that family of origin is important, but it is not more important than origin of family (God). Remember who you are? You are a child of God (from the first chapter of this workbook).

Before You Continue—Family of Origin Parenting Styles

1) How did your parents discipline you?

2) Was it effective in communicating who you are as child of God? If it wasn't, how are you changing this in your parenting?

We say that origin of family is more important than family of origin because if we forget who we are as children of God, then the wounds (or difficulties) from our family of origin will fight hard to give us a false identity, and in our brokenness we sometimes believe this false identity.

Wounds From Our Family of Origin—a Clinical Example

This was the case with Jim's client, Linda. She told Jim that her first memory was being thrown across the room by a physically abusive parent. That is a huge, powerful wound that tried to give Linda a false identity by reminding her that she was no good, not worthy of love, and not worthy of respectful treatment. We all have wounds like this, whether they are brutal, like Linda's, or less severe, like emotional neglect or being yelled at by a parent.

Linda eventually married an abusive husband because she listened to the wounds that gave her a false identity. That's when Jim met her. They worked for quite some time to heal this false identity. They also worked on allowing God to tell her who she truly is as a precious daughter of the King. This required extensive therapy and openness on Linda's part.

She's now out of that abusive relationship and doing much better, although when stress is high she still sometimes believes she's that little girl who doesn't deserve love. But by focusing daily on her true identity as a daughter of God, there has been healing in her life. Linda's story, to some degree, is also our story.

We all have hurts and wounds in our past or present. These wounds want to give us a false identity. Because this false identity is from a wound, it won't be too attractive, and it can influence many major decisions we make. In Linda's case she actually married an abusive husband because she had been listening to her family of origin wounds and following this false identity for years. Our task as parents is to rebuke the lie and to focus on the truth of who we are as children of God.

Listen to the Word, Not to the Wound

When we remember who we are (a child of the King) we see that the wounds from our family of origin, or hurts from the present, have already been redeemed by the One who loves to redeem, Christ our Lord. We may still have to process these hurts with someone we trust, but be assured that they're redeemed because you are a child of the King, and the wounds were too late. We need to listen to the Word and not to the wounds. Let's consider this in more depth.

The Word reminds us that "For it was you who formed my inward parts; you knit me together in my mother's womb" (Ps. 139:13). That psalm is beautiful, freeing, and true! If God created us in our mother's womb, then the wounds that happen in that womb or outside that womb are too late to give you an identity! Our wounds will try hard all our life to give us a false identity, but they need not fool us; we need to focus on the truth and remind ourselves who we are as children of the King.

We also need to focus on how we have a Brother who loves to heal our wounds by His own wounds and resurrection. Jesus does this healing through an amazing process that takes place in the brain.

We have evidence showing that when we bring up an old hurt in our family of origin (or any old hurt) and edit that hurt with the compassion of another person listening, this can actually lead to a sort of re-wiring of the orbital frontal cortex, a part of the brain involved in emotional maturity. So as we share our stories of pain from our family of origin (or any hurt) with a brother or sister in Christ who listens and edits that hurt with compassion, this can lead to profound healing. Christ desires that we heal our wounds from our family of origin so we do not pass them on to our children.

Once a hurt is healed, Christ wants to resurrect it and bring good from it! Christ our Lord not only heals our wounds but brings good from them through His resurrection and Spirit working in our lives. Obviously, our wounds are still difficult and may take years to heal, as in Linda's case. But to know and tell ourselves that our wounds do not give us an identity and to know that God can bring good from our wounds is the Good News.

The Power of Romans 8:28

Romans 8:28 is a good reason to get out of bed in the morning. It sums up the entire Bible in a poignant and empowering truth: "We know that all things work together for good for those who love God and are called according to His purpose." If you haven't pondered this verse recently, please re-read it and let it sink in. This is a divine promise from God that when we have wounds, either from our family of origin or from the present, God wants to heal them and actually bring good from them. We have seen that personally and professionally for years, and we are sure you have too. One example from our marriage powerfully testifies to Romans 8:28.

An Example of Romans 8:28 From Our Life

We met in a graduate Scripture class. Jim used to change his seat in that class so that he could see Maureen. (He probably needed to pay closer attention to the professor—Sorry, Father Luke!). After we met, we would sometimes think about if God was calling us to marriage and how many children we would like to have. Jim had it all figured out one day in graduate school (he still has the notes) that we could have seven children. We both love children and that is how many children Maureen's parents have. But life had other plans.

We were married in 1995 and wanted to share our love by having children. But the road to parenthood was arduous and complex. We went through years of infertility, trips to specialists, different medications, and uncertainty. When we would finally conceive we had several miscarriages. We were not sure if we could even carry a child to term. Those were dark days in our life, and we thank God for the light of faith, family, friends, and a supportive faith community. Now looking back, we can see that God loved us so much that He didn't want that pain (or any suffering in our life) to be squandered. God was faithful in bringing about new life from those death experiences.

Many times through the years couples have shared with us their pain of infertility or miscarriage. They did this not because of what we have, but because of what the Holy Spirit does by bringing resurrections from all our deaths. We are now able to bring hope and consolation to other couples by the same consolation that the Spirit gave us. That is the resurrection cycle, and it will continue until the Kingdom comes for those who are open to it. These are just a few ways in our marriage and parenting that God has been faithful to His promise in Romans 8:28. Take some time now to reflect on these themes in your life.

Before You Continue—The Word vs. Wounds

1) Are there specific wounds in your life from your family of origin or from the present that try to give you a false identity?

2) Do you listen to the lies of those wounds, or have you learned to focus on the truth of who you are as a child of God? In other words, do you listen to the Word or to the wounds?

3) Do you feel there are family of origin wounds, or other wounds in your life, that need healing? If so, please take some time to contact your pastor.

4) What are your "Romans 8:28 moments?" In other words, when you look back on the difficulties you've been through, where has the Holy Spirit brought good from them? How do these help your parenting today?

Prayer About Family of Origin and Origin of Family

All good and ever present God, You continue to bring forth new life from all the death experiences I go through. I thank You for this Resurrection cycle. Send Your Spirit into my heart, mind, and relationships today so that I can trust Your healing power for the wounds in my life. May Your Spirit heal and bring hope by teaching me that all things do work for the good when we love You. I make this prayer through Christ our Lord in the power of the Holy Spirit. Amen.

Eighth Daily Dozen: Don't Buy Society's Lies   **8**

"I am the way, and the truth, and the life." —John 14:6

Unfortunately we have a tendency in our brokenness to forget that Christ is the truth. Thus, we tend to listen to and follow the glut of lies that our society promotes. There are so many lies in our culture when it comes to parenting that it would be impossible to list them all here. But when we critically consider our 21st century world in light of Jesus' statement above, "I am the way, and the truth, and the life," three core lies become apparent: consumerism, relativism, and low moral expectations. Consumerism as the way, a relative approach to truth, and a life compromised by low moral expectations pose enormous challenges to us in our vocation as Catholic parents.

Consumerism

Jesus tells us, "I am the way." But the consumer culture in which we live would have us believe otherwise. The "way" in our money-oriented society is to buy, to acquire, to consume, to get more, to have the newest and the best. It's a system that feeds on the human weakness of greed. It knows that we are never satisfied with this thing (even this NEW thing!), so it's able to sell us even more new things. It never ends, and that's exactly how it's designed to work. But Jesus, being both man and God, knows both our human condition and our thirst for the divine. He knows that things in and of themselves will never satisfy us, and that only He can. When considered against the eternal promise of life in Christ, the fleeting value of acquiring possessions becomes pretty obvious.

Consumerism also infects our parenting because when we buy into it, parenting becomes a matter of material stuff and not about the spiritual realities around us. We lose sight of the eternal for the temporal.

Of course we need things when raising children and these will vary from situation to situation. But overall, too many of us have too much stuff and we buy too much stuff for our children. What can we do about it? First, we need to pray about what God is calling us to do when it comes to buying gifts (Christmas, Easter, birthdays, etc.). We love the idea of purchasing three gifts for each child on Christmas because that is the number of gifts that Jesus received. Then, the money saved could be donated to a local "Toys for Tots" or Salvation Army, or it could be given to Heifer International (www. heifer.org), which invests the money to help families learn to help themselves.

Another obvious area of consumerism is the types of vehicles we purchase. Do we buy high consumption vehicles because of status? Or do we not care what others will think and purchase more practical vehicles? What type of clothes do we buy for ourselves and our children? With clothes and vehicles alone we could save thousands of dollars and donate the money to on-going charities that work to empower the poor. There are many other physical consumerist questions that you can pray about as well, and we hope you'll take the time to do that so you can hear God calling you to be counter-cultural in this area of parenting.

When we pray and talk about this we can see the value in living simply, so that others may simply live, as Mother Teresa said. We also model for our children the importance of delayed gratification (I don't have to have everything I want right now, and there is value in waiting) as well as the Catholic social teaching of the preferential option for the poor. Simply put, this teaching insists that the poor have a right to a share in our possessions and our wealth, since everything is ultimately from God.

Before You Continue

These questions aren't meant to be shame-based, but to examine our habits.

1) Are you prayerfully trying to live simply so that others may simply live?

2) If not, what are some areas that you could reduce your spending on?

3) Once you have become less of a consumer you may have more financial resources to share with others in need. Besides your local church, what other non-profit organization do you think God is calling you to support?

Spiritual Consumerism

Consumerism is not just physical; it's also spiritual. Spiritual consumerism is the notion that I choose what is right for me spiritually and opt to participate only when there is something in it for me.

Maureen encountered this attitude in her work in pastoral ministry and faith formation at our parish. She recalls answering the phone one day in early September and being told, "I'm looking for a parish since I'm new to the area, and I'm calling to see what your faith formation program has to offer." While it's important to find the right fit in seeking a parish, this comment sadly seemed to sum up how too many parishioners view faith formation (or other programs at the parish): I go to the parish or register there so I can get my kids into faith formation (so they can receive the sacraments, ultimately), not so much because it is my faith home where I worship every week.

And on that note, we've probably all heard the person who explains their lack of weekly worship with the parish by saying that they can find God out in nature. We delight that people can find God at the lake and in the woods. We love watching the sun dance on the lake during a beautiful summer day or finding God during a walk in the woods, hiking, mountain climbing, biking, talking to a friend, getting lost in a leaf, or walking on the beach.

But the question about weekly public worship is not about where I can find God, which can be a form of spiritual consumerism. It's about what God wants me to do as His creature. God created me; I didn't create God. God tells me what to do; not the other way around. God wants me to worship publicly every week (at least), and the sad truth is that many of our fellow parishioners have slowly bought into the lie of spiritual consumerism. Customers, by definition, choose whether, when, and where to purchase. The most important principle in consumerism is that everything is up to me. I make every decision based upon "what I'm getting out of it." When a thing no longer entertains me, interests me, or serves me, I discard it, abandon it, or give up on it. When we apply that to our Catholic faith we come up with some very wrong—and far-reaching—conclusions.

One example is thinking we no longer need to attend church every week. Obviously, this won't be an absolute, as in the situation where we are ill or a child is ill and there's no childcare. Those are meant to be the exception and not the norm.

Weekly worship is one of the Ten Commandments ("Keep Holy the Lord's day") and it's re-iterated in the New Testament as well. In the Acts of the Apostles we read how the early Christians gathered regularly to worship God as a community. From the very beginning of the Christian Church, public worship has been central to the experience of being a member of the Body of Christ. In addition, it is one of the seven precepts of the Catholic Church, which lay out for us the "indispensable minimum in the spirit of prayer and moral effort, in the growth of God and neighbour" (CCC, #2041-2).

Another way to look at this question of weekly church attendance is through the lens of activities for our children. When our children are in extra-curricular activities there's an expectation that they will participate in all of the requirements of that activity. This may include purchasing equipment, daily practice, selling things to raise funds, obeying the rules or following the coach or leader. If we only applied that sense of belonging to our Catholic identity, our parishes would come alive in America!

Before You Continue

These questions aren't meant to be shame-based, but to examine our habits.

1) Has the cancer of spiritual consumerism (thinking you don't need weekly public worship, for example) harmed you and your family?

2) If you answered "yes" to that question, please take a few minutes to pray about re-connecting with your local parish.

Relativism

Jesus says, "I am the truth." Such a bold statement directly conflicts with the cultural currents that tell us, "If it feels good, do it," "Anything goes," and "As long as I'm not hurting anyone, it's OK."

We live in a world that claims there are virtually no objective truths, a world very far removed from the people of Jesus' time. The Ten Commandments together with the New Law Jesus gave us spell out in no uncertain terms the truths of a life lived in harmony with God and centered on Christ.

Simply stated, relativism is the idea that there are no real constants or truths in the world and that one opinion is as valid as the next. You can't judge me because my opinions are just as worthwhile as yours, no matter how lacking in logic they may be. The whole tidal wave of "spirituality" that we see in self-help books smacks of relativism.

Many relationship gurus tell us that we need to follow our feelings because that is where "happiness" is. When parents buy this lie the consequences are devastating. We have children who are being raised without a clear understanding that there is such a thing as the truth . . . His name is Jesus the Christ.

Some parents say, "But life is not always black and white. There are lots of grey areas." We totally agree. The problem is that when we come to a grey area (an area where we are not sure what to do) we need to go back to the black and white (the truths that we know). Unfortunately we have not been teaching our children these truths as much as we used to, so that when they come up against grey areas they no longer have the safety of these truths. Some of our children no longer know that there are objective truths such as faith, hope, love (not lust), respect, honor, and obedience. We can start combating this lie of relativism by spending time with our children and teaching age-appropriate critical thinking skills based on the truth. Jesus says, "I am the truth." We need to go back to the black and white.

One such skill that we teach our children is to judge behavior, but not people. Because of relativism, the word "judge" gets a bad rap. But in the Gospel of John, Jesus tells us, "Do not judge by appearances, but judge with right judgment" (Jn. 7:24).

Many places in Scripture warn of judging others. This passage from John acts as an invitation to judge actions and attitudes, but not people. We can't judge people because that is not our place; only God sees the heart. But because God has given us each a brain, we need to judge actions and attitudes so that we can see how to prayerfully respond to them. Refraining from judging people doesn't mean approving of (or turning a blind eye to) their every behavior.

Another area where we see relativism in parenting is in the area of respect. We find it troubling to see the way today's children show such little respect for authority, which is again due to relativism. We do our children and our world a huge service by using appropriate leverages to teach our children to respect themselves and others. We always invite parents to correct a disrespectful attitude or action, even if it is a "small one," such as rolling eyes or sarcasm. Jesus tells us that if we are trustworthy with the small things in life, we will be trustworthy with larger things. So, we need to stop disrespectful behavior as soon as it starts.

Before You Continue

These questions aren't meant to be shame-based, but to examine our habits.

1) Are there areas in your parenting that buy the lie of relativism?

2) If so, what are these areas and what can you do today about them?

3) Are there truths you were taught as a child that you have abandoned for a more relativistic approach to life? If so, what are they? How might God be inviting you to re-examine these truths?

4) Do you use and teach the distinction of judging actions and attitudes, but not people? If not, what do you think about that distinction?

5) There is a familiar saying, "Love the sinner, hate the sin." How does this distinction help teach children that it's good and holy to use their brain to avoid some situations in life?

Low Moral Expectations

Jesus said, "I am the life." Sadly, we live in a culture of death; a culture that prizes individual "choice" over the very value of human life, a culture that encourages promiscuity and thus profoundly devalues the holiness of sexuality; a culture that tears at the fabric of family life by questioning the essential integrity of marriage. Much of this follows from the relativism we just discussed. Relativism gives way to low moral expectations, a particularly serious issue for Catholic parents. We have a tendency today as parents to not expect good things from our children—especially our teenaged children. We see this low moral expectation in the way our children talk, their behaviors, the way they dress, etc. The one aspect of low moral expectation that we want to discuss more in depth is sexuality.

We could begin by quoting data from The Centers for Disease Control (CDC). The CDC reports that "at least 50% of sexually active people will have genital human papillomavirus (HPV) at some time in their lives." To be sure, the CDC says much more about HPV. But that 50% is a staggering number! Citing data from a secular organization like the CDC is helpful up to a point.

Yes, these statistics support everything the Catholic Church has taught since the beginning: that sexual expression should be reserved for marriage. But statistics shouldn't be our starting point.

Rather, we should begin with the very words of Jesus: "I am the life." If we desire life in its fullness for our children and ourselves we must teach them Catholic wisdom regarding sexuality, which exposes the lies of our present-day culture. One prevalent lie is the presumption that our teens are going to be sexually active. Obviously, there are no guarantees, but if we start early and discuss the wholeness and beauty of sexuality, we believe we can minimize the odds that our children will fall into this destructive and potentially lethal lie.

We hear a lie that says something like this to our teens, "If you're going to experiment sexually, use safe sex." What a lie! There is no such thing as "safe sex." Sex is a complicated reality even for adults in a Catholic marriage. Every act of sexuality is, by definition, vulnerable, because in sexual acts we give ourselves away to another person, so there is no "safe sex." Our discussion of sexuality with our children needs to happen early and often. **It's no longer the "big talk;" rather it's a whole lot of little, Christ-centered talks.**

Moreover, before you discuss this gift in life, make sure that you have prayed about it and thought about it yourself, and that you are comfortable with your own body. We recommend talking to children about sexuality around the age of seven or younger and using age appropriate language. At this age many children are already discussing it, and we would rather have our children learn about sexuality from their parents instead of their seven-year old peers.

There's another reason why earlier can be better. The next time you go through a grocery store checkout line, look at the garbage that is available for our children to see, right at their eye level: tabloids with scantily clad women and men talking about how to have a good orgasm. Right there by the candy. We live in a sex-saturated culture and we need to understand how God created sexuality and how God wants us to talk to our children about it.

Tips on the "Sex Talk"

The best tip on discussing sexuality is to make sure that you have a healthy Catholic outlook on sexuality. God created us beautifully, and that is the starting point of a healthy Christian sexuality.

The image Jim taught kids while doing youth ministry is from his childhood, when his family raised dogs. Every year when their female dogs were ready to mate, they would watch all the male dogs come running. You couldn't tell those male dogs "Bad doggy!" because those dogs were living by their instincts, exactly the way God created them to be. Humans, on the other hand, have a brain that can process our instincts and think about our thinking. And if we are to live the way God created us, we can actually talk about our sex drive rather than being enslaved by our hormones. That's a countercultural thought that needs to be discussed. We can harness our sexuality through prayer, exercise, talking about it, journaling about it, appreciating beauty every day, and by understanding the concept that love waits.

Use age-appropriate information and answer only the questions your children ask. For example, if a child asks, "Daddy, where did I come from?" instead of choking on your coffee and trying to discuss sexuality, ask them, "What do you mean?" The child might say, "What town was I born in?" or "What state was I born in?"

This actually happens, so we want to make sure that the questions they ask are really about sexuality.

When describing body parts we encourage using real terms: use the words "vagina" and "penis"; they are not bad words. When your child is old enough you can use the word "intercourse" and let them know that it is so good and beautiful that God wants us to wait until we are married. God created us beautifully and wonderfully and we don't need to have shame when we discuss this great gift.

Normalize some curiosity. It's quite normal for children to have some sexual curiosity. If you find your son or daughter experimenting by themselves, don't use shame. Instead let your child know that God created them beautifully and wonderfully and that our sexuality is so good and beautiful that God wants us to use it only in special ways in marriage.

Jim was working with one parent who found her teenaged child masturbating, and this parent wondered what to do. Even though it happens frequently in our sex-saturated culture, masturbating doesn't have to happen. Jim asked this parent how often the child receives hugs, because usually when he is counseling a child who masturbates he encourages more hugging with the parents and more snuggle time (if age appropriate and child-approved). It's a good idea to think about what you want to teach your child about masturbation.

We have a few observations, based on Jim's experience as a Christian therapist, that we would make regarding masturbating. In all of Jim's years as a therapist, he has never talked to a spouse who likes it when their spouse masturbates; on the contrary, he has talked to numerous spouses who despise it.

The other point to think about masturbation is that when a person is doing it, they are probably not thinking about an inanimate or neutral object—it is indeed a sexual act. Jesus tells us in the Gospel that if one looks lustfully at another they have already committed adultery (Mt 5:28). Christ tells us this because orgasm is ideally meant for sharing and communicating love and life to a spouse, not to oneself. But in a sex-saturated culture we tend to buy the lie that "What I do in my bedroom is my business; I'm not hurting anyone." The Bible disagrees.

In the midst of his profound discourse on how Christians are all connected by Baptism, Paul tells us "If one part of the body suffers, all the other parts suffer with it" (Cor.12: 26). When we realize that sin is the most profound type of suffering, then we see that sin is social. So, according to the Word of God, what I do in my bedroom does impact you, and vice-versa.

A word of caution: Do not use shame when thinking or talking about masturbation or any sexual issue; it will only harm and bring more damage. Always talk about how God loves us and desires that we learn the innate beauty of our sexuality and that we can harness our sexual desires. Also, talk about the freedom that Christ offers. Galatians 4:7 reveals to us the supremacy of our identity in Christ: "So you are no longer a slave but a child, and if a child then also an heir, through God." We were not created for slavery of any kind (sexual, financial, emotional, etc.) but we were created for freedom in Christ.

Another key to these sex talks is to keep both parents very active in the process. In fact, we think it's great when fathers can describe to their 9-or 10-year old daughters what will happen to their bodies when their menstruation cycle starts. If fathers don't understand the complexities of the feminine cycle, we encourage them to learn about the hormones involved and the different phases that happen each month. This will not only help them with their parenting but will help their marriage as well. The more Dad is involved with positive validation and his time, the less likely children will fall into difficult sexual traps.

Anyone with any sexual shame, addiction, or past abuse needs to know that healing is possible and that God wants to love us into new life. Jim has seen that happen through the power of the Holy Spirit, so have hope because you are God's child. If you need healing in this area of sexuality there are Christian therapists who have helped others see and live that freedom.

When your son or daughter is around the wonderful age of 10 or 11, go on an overnight chastity retreat and give your son or daughter a chastity ring as part of that retreat. There are many models for this time. Pray about which one fits you best. Children seem to be more open to listening to this important message around the age of 11 or 12, compared to the early teens.

Before You Continue

These questions aren't meant to be shame-based but to examine our habits.

1) Who taught you about sexuality? Was it positive? If it wasn't positive, what can you change when you teach your children about this beautiful gift?

2) Are you comfortable with your own sexuality? Why or why not?

3) What does Galatians 4:7 ("We are no longer slaves, but we are children of God") mean to your sexuality?

4) Have you talked to your children yet about sexuality? If not, what tips from this chapter can you use to help with those little talks?

More Tips to Teach Healthy Christian Sexuality Through Different Ages and Stages

What is Healthy Christian Sexuality?

It begins by understanding the nature of human sexuality and by following the simple yet powerful instructions that God gives us in His Holy Word. God loves us. We are created in God's image and likeness (Gen. 1:27). There was no shame in the garden—only perfect unity with God and each other. Because God is good, and we were created in His image and likeness, we are good. Before the fall of humanity, God blessed the man and the woman and told them to be fruitful and multiply (Gen.1:28). So, God blessed them (the "blessing" was their marriage) and only then did God say, "Be fruitful and multiply."

The order God set up is to have a marriage between one man and one woman first, and only after that marriage was sexual activity allowed and blessed. This is the order God set up. Sexuality is a huge gift that God has created, and like all gifts, it must be used in the proper context. If we follow the instructions that God gives us, we see that authentic human sexuality can only be truly experienced and enjoyed in a marriage between one man and one woman (the "blessing" of God). God delights in the appropriate use of human sexuality when we obey the creator of sexuality (God).

When we step outside of that holy order and have sexual activity outside of marriage, we are violating the very nature of sexuality itself, because this is not how God created it to work. Thus, it will never lead to true fulfillment. Following this sacred order that God created becomes much harder because of sin.

We read in Genesis Chapter 3 about the first sin entering the world, and the holy order that God set up was not obeyed. But because God loves us, in the fullness of time, He sent us His only Son to reconcile us back to the Father through His life, death, resurrection, and sending of the Holy Spirit.

Thus, healthy Christian sexuality means that we're redeemed sons and daughters of God. We are good and holy and our bodies are sacred: "Do you not know that your body is a temple of the Holy Spirit, within you, which you have from God, and that you are not your own? For you were bought with a price; therefore glorify God in your body" (I Cor. 6: 19-20).

How do we "glorify God in our bodies?" One way is to recapture the holy order set up by God himself in Genesis and trying to live this out and teaching our children. But we first need to understand it ourselves. Attitude reflects leadership; always has, always will. In no other area is this truer than in sexuality. The best thing we can do to start to teach our children healthy Christian sexuality is to first get comfortable with our own skin, with our own temples of the Holy Spirit, our bodies. If you have personal issues of sexual shame, or do not view your body (including sexuality) as a temple of the Holy Spirit, we invite you to really accept the Gospel truth of the goodness of your body before you try to teach it to your children.

Many parents we work with have opened up the gift of sexuality early in their life, or they had their beautiful gift of sexuality violated by someone else's sin (e.g., rape or sexual abuse). In either case, it's never too late for healing and wholeness in Christ Jesus. Jesus sends us His spirit of power so that we may know that we are no longer slaves (to any past personal sin, or sin done to us), but we are sons and daughters of God, and thus, we are heirs of God! (Gal. 4:7). You may need to talk with your pastor, a Christian coach, or Christian therapist to heal these wounds. Please take this first step seriously. In order to pass on to our children a healthy view of Christian sexuality, we first need to have a healthy view of Christian sexuality.

You may also need help with your children's use of the Internet. Visit www.covenanteyes.com for some of the most powerful software available to help with accountability and monitoring Internet use.

Before You Continue

1) What are some positive, holy views of sexuality that you were taught in your family of origin?

2) What are some more difficult areas that may need healing when it comes to sexuality so that you don't pass these difficulties on to your children?

3) Do you have any "private sins" that you need to repent of in order to restore healthy order in your life?

Recognize that some sexual habits can be very addicting, and professional help might be needed. Also, recognize that you are so loved by God, and that the Holy Spirit is more powerful than any addiction! A great free Christian resource is www.settingcaptivesfree.com. Two specifically Catholic resources are: www.integrityrestored.com and www.reclaimsexualhealth.com.

Healthy Christian sexuality must be taught in our homes at an early age by lovingly and authentically weaving it into everything we do. In fact, some of the best sex talks we have had with our children happen over lunch or in the van running here and there. But that's all based on how we as parents see ourselves first. We're very non-shaming, Gospel-based when it comes to our sexuality and teaching that sexuality to our children. Today's children are exposed to much more information about sex than we were, growing up in the early 1970s. Our children will learn about sexuality from someone, and we want that someone to be a loving parent who understands the goodness and beauty of sexuality.

Our "entertainment" also teaches our children explicitly what the body is for: pleasure. We need to stop that half-truth (and all half-truths in our world) with the full truth. We parents are still the number one influence on our children, so we need to start early to teach our children healthy, Catholic-based sexuality: that the body is not just for pleasure, but it's a temple of the Holy Spirit (and that can be very pleasurable in the right context of a Christian marriage, following the holy order God set up from the beginning).

This is where having a sign on our childrens' bedroom door, or the bathroom mirror, that tells them "I am a child of God. Treat me lovingly" really helps. As they grow older we can keep talking about how men and women should treat each other "lovingly" and not "lustingly." These are distinctions that we can make as they get older. To "lust" over someone is to make them an object, and people can never be objects; people are always subjects.

Talking to Our Children About Healthy Christian Sexuality by Age

We want to preface this section by pointing out that children are formed by their total environment (no news there). Particularly in attitudes toward sexuality, they are influenced by the media they consume. For this reason, it is vitally important that you monitor their intake in books, TV, radio, YouTube and other online sources. Be proactive in introducing them to quality Catholic media, including books about the saints, music and movies with Christian themes, and media that uphold and promote the values you are trying to teach them. It is a big job, no doubt. But just as you try to provide them with healthy nutrition for their bodies, it's even more important to nourish them spiritually.

Conception–Age 2

The primary task at this point is to make sure we as parents have done the necessary healing work in our own lives so that we understand the sacred order that God created in Genesis and we understand that we're no longer slaves. We need to live in the authentic freedom of God, which is how we were created by God to be. If you're not living in that beautiful freedom as a son or daughter of God, please get some healing so that past hurts and wounds won't be passed on to your children.

Ages 2-4

At this age, start telling your children that their bodies are good and God created them to be "temples of the Holy Spirit" (I Cor. 6:19). Yes, you can teach your children the word "temple." If kids can say "To infinity and beyond" we can certainly teach them the word "temple"! Tell them that a temple is where God lives, and God lives in their bodies, and their bodies are good!

• It's important to start early so we can normalize their questions, and also to ensure that children hear the truth about sexuality from their parents, their "first teachers in the ways of faith" (as the Rite of Baptism states).

• When bathing children this age, teach them that their bodies are good, and that girls have a vagina and boys have a penis. Tell them that their vagina or penis is good, just like their hands and fingers are. But teach them the difference: the penis and vagina are so good and so special that they are "private parts," so we need to pray and talk about who can see them.

• Teach good touch and bad touch. Teach them that only Mommy and Daddy or a doctor (with Mommy or Daddy present) should touch their private parts. If anyone else touches their private parts, they should tell Mom or Dad or a trusted adult. Teach them that when they get older and if they're married, their husband or wife will be able to touch their private parts during special times. Do this all frequently during bath time as they ask questions about their body. Most boys mature more slowly than girls so the time-frame can be slightly different for them. But the truth is the same: their bodies are good. Use age-appropriate information with proper names for body parts. Don't use slang words; the word "penis" is not a bad word, nor is the word "vagina." If you need to, practice those words so you don't blush when you say them.

• Each day, through your daily prayer and talk time, teach them that they're good and are temples of the Holy Spirit and that God loves them very much. When they ask normal questions about how boys and girls are different, talk about it factually, and with wonder and awe. When they ask where they came from, tell them "God created your beautiful souls and Mommy and Daddy helped create your beautiful bodies."

Ages 5-6

Their curiosity continues to grow and they may touch their bodies, which could simply be curiosity, like how their hands work or how their tummy works. If you see this going on, never use shame. Always tell your five and six-year olds that their bodies are good and holy (as they have heard because you have been doing that since conception)!

• Tell them also that curiosity is good, but with questions about the body it's best to talk to Mommy or Daddy. When they talk to you, let them know that their penis or vagina is holy and private, never to be touched by anyone except a doctor (when Mom or Dad are with them), and sometimes by Mom and Dad. Remind them again about good touch and bad touch. We have to remember that this information takes a long time to settle into their growing brains. Be patient and be Christ-centered.

• When you pray with your five-and six-year-olds, pray about how good and holy their bodies are, how God loves them, and how God has great plans for them. Unlike some groups who want to teach five old year olds that it's good and "healthy" to masturbate, our Catholic faith does not. We want to keep our five and six year-olds innocent by monitoring what they watch, listen to, read, and who they play with.

Ages 7-8
For both girls and boys:

Teach them during their teen years that they'll need more sleep (9.5 – 10 hours a night. Plant that seed early on). We're convinced that many teen-aged issues are due to sleep deprivation, too much screentime, and their peer group (show me your friends; we will show you your future . . . true for teens and adults)! This is why we don't have TVs in our bedrooms—another good habit to start early on.

• Start to teach them that as they get older, their bodies will start to change and go through puberty. Puberty is a good thing and God will bless their body (a temple of the Holy Spirit) by changing it slowly. Girls will get taller, breasts will start to develop, and they will start to get hair around the vaginal area and under their arms. Boys will get more muscular and grow facial hair and more hair around their penis and under-arms, and their voice may fluctuate as it becomes deeper.

• With girls: teach them about beginner bras and how they can wear them when their breasts start to develop. It's good to talk about them before you buy them. When they're ready to buy a beginner bra, celebrate this! If your daughter is comfortable with it, have her go shopping with Mom and Dad and go out to eat afterwards. Celebrate the fact that their little bodies are changing slowly, just as God designed. Tell them this is a few years away, but continue to assure them it's good and holy and they can be respectful teenagers (speak that future into being)!

• With boys: teach them that they need to be very respectful of themselves and others, especially girls. Don't let them get into any negative bullying habits (just because "boys will be boys"); that's not healthy Christian sexuality! Teach your boys at this age that they are called by God to protect life and to cherish themselves and others. Teach them that when they reach puberty, they will be awesome, respectful teenagers (speak that future into being with boys as well)!

Ages 9-10

Continue teaching them how good their bodies are and more about how the body works. Teach them about egg cells and sperm cells and how we all started out as one little cell, when one sperm cell met one egg cell. Continue to remind them about puberty and the goodness of being a teenager.

• Remind them that when they're teens they will be respectful and good, and that their bodies are temples of the Holy Spirit. Teach them, and continue to teach them, that if anyone says "I love you" and starts to touch any of their private areas, that's not love until they're married because that sort of touching is reserved for a special relationship between one man and one woman, which we call the Sacrament of Marriage.

• Start to teach them that they won't get an adult brain until they're about 24 years old. That's why many parents won't let teens go out with the opposite sex alone on a "date." This is not just some old-fashioned notion; it's a biological fact. Remind them frequently of this biological fact (for more, see the information about Catholic dating at the end of this chapter).

• More biology for this age group: teach them about hormones and how hormones are messengers in the blood system that help our bodies do many things.

• At this age remind them that when puberty starts they will have to shower more often (every other day, and eventually everyday) because their bodies will produce more sweat. Teach them about using deodorant daily as well.

• Dads should be very involved with teaching their 9- or 10-year daughters about their cycle, at an early age, with child-appropriate language. If dads don't know about the female cycle, we invite them to learn about it so they can teach their sons and daughters.

• With boys ages 10 and 11, remind them how their bodies will change during puberty: they will get taller, more muscular, and hairy, and may smell different (hence the daily shower or bath). Also teach them about hormones: there are many hormones, which are messengers in the blood—that's all they are—like a postal delivery system. Tell them specifically about testosterone and how it will increase when they're teens and will cause these changes.

• Also at ages 10 and 11, teach boys about erections and that just because the body has an erection doesn't mean that it needs to lead to an ejaculation. Again, there's no shame here; it's how a teenaged male body works. (You may need to teach them the word "ejaculation" as well—it's a special power that God gives men to co-create new life and it's meant to be used in marriage during intercourse.) Teach them that their penis is good, just like their hands are good. Teach them that with manhood comes responsibility. God desires that we use our hands, and the rest of our bodies, to do good things, not bad things. Hands can be used in a great way to help Mom and Dad unload dishes or help a neighbor. But the hand can also be used in a bad way: stealing, cheating in school, hitting someone, etc. The penis is similar. It's used by the body in a great way: to get rid of waste, in the form of urine. It can also be used to create new life, which is meant to be done in a marriage when we follow the holy order set up in Genesis by our Creator.

• We want to use our bodies in good ways because they're temples of the Holy Spirit. Teach your children one great way to do this is through marriage and creating new life through "intercourse," when a husband and wife both agree to come together to share their married love. Sexuality and intercourse are such special gifts we want to save it (keep the gift wrapped) until marriage, and follow God's design in Genesis.

• Teach boys about "nocturnal" (or night) ejaculations and how they're the body's way of letting us know that something very special is happening, and they're a holy gift. This gift is a special responsibility and it means they're becoming men. But, like all good gifts, it needs to be used wisely and never abused. With great gifts comes great responsibility.

• Teach males that they don't have to be controlled by this new experience, and teach them that the more they are able to get enough good sleep, the more they aren't exposed to sexually explicit material (porn), and the more they focus on their goodness as a son of God, puberty is a blessed time, and they will be respectful men of God. Teach young boys that an erection doesn't need to lead to an ejaculation.

• For single moms, it can be a good idea to ask your pastor, another youth minister, or a trusted Christian man in your church to help you by having this discussion with your son. A trusted Christian uncle or other Christian man who feels comfortable supporting this idea can be helpful in teaching your son what it means to be a son of God.

• When boys and girls are 10 and 11, continue the conversation about how good their bodies are and how they'll change during puberty: do this during prayer time, during meal time or anytime you're together as family, and make sure that these talks include both Mom and Dad. Try to normalize this conversation because God created us, and there's no shame in our bodies when we live in God's law of love.

• Teach boys and girls at 10 and 11 about the three primary hormones in the female body during puberty: progesterone, estrogen, and oxytocin. Oxytocin is the "bonding hormone" that women experience after a baby is born, and this hormone also surges during puberty in young women. That's one of the reason girls tend to be "touchy" during their teen years. You'll rarely see a group of boys walking arm in arm down the school hallway, because they don't have nearly the amount of oxytocin that girls have.

• This is why Dads and Moms need to hug their teen daughters frequently! Teen girls need to bond physically with someone and we pray that they will bond with us and other safe girls, instead of with boys, who tend to misread this need to bond as an invitation to sexual activity. If a girl, who just wants a hug because of high oxytocin levels, hugs a boy and the boy doesn't understand that the girl just wants a hug, this can be misunderstood by the boy and can lead to him acting on his primary hormone (testosterone). That's one reason why we teach our young men that just because they get an erection, it doesn't have to lead to an ejaculation. These lessons are critically important, and if enough parents teach this it could lower the number of date rapes in our culture.

• At 10 and 11 we keep adding to the knowledge base: more about the female and male cycle, more about menstruation, pregnancy, and even introducing the idea of "intercourse" and how God desires that we keep intercourse and the beauty of sexuality for marriage by following God's design.

• Regarding menstruation, tell boys and girls that although it might not feel good, it's still a good thing. Once a cycle is "regular," which can take a while during the teen years, it happens every 30 days or so. It doesn't feel good, but it's so good for the uterus to shed and cleanse its lining each month. If the uterus doesn't shed its lining, disease can settle in, which can lead to other problems. The stomach does something similar, except the cycle of replacing the lining of the stomach lasts just about 3-4 days and isn't painful.

• Because our bodies are so good, sexuality is a gift, and the only time we should open that gift is after we create a sacramental marriage. Recognize that there's a special openness during the ages of 10–12 that we need to capitalize on!

• If we can continue to impress upon our children the truth about the goodness of sexuality before their teen years, it can bear fruit when they're older. This is when it's good to start to "date" your children more often, listen attentively, get involved in their life, and maybe start the habit of a yearly retreat. If you start the yearly retreat when they're 10 or 11, they may indeed want to continue it into their teen years. That's what we have seen with our teenaged daughters, and it's a huge blessing to us and them to go together on retreat every year.

• Talk about the discharge that may be happening and how your daughter may see some in her underwear. Tell her this is all very normal and with no shame so that she knows what is going on before it happens.

• In addition, a dad could also take his son out to dinner when the boy starts to mature. Celebrating passages is very important. It's very empowering for a Mom and Dad to tell their son and daughter "I believe in you" when they're teenagers.

• Boys usually experiment with masturbation, as do some girls. Talk about that in a non-shaming way. Shame will only distract from the life-long lesson that you have been teaching your child that they are "temples of the Holy Spirit." To boys, talk about how God loves them and that the act of ejaculation was created by God to bring new life into the world and to draw him closer to a wife. Because it's so beautiful, intercourse and the gift of sexuality are designed to be shared with a spouse only in the Sacrament of Marriage.

• To girls who are masturbating, talk about how an orgasm is such a great blessing that ideally, we want to save it for marriage. Again, never talk about sexual issues in a shaming way. Remember that just because there has been some experimenting with masturbation, this doesn't mean it has to lead to addiction. That said, an orgasm floods the brain with dopamine, serotonin, oxytocin (and many other feel-good neurotransmitters) so it can lead to addiction. If you think your son or daughter has any unhealthy patterns of sexual experimentation, we always recommend Christian counseling.

• At age 13 and 14 we hope that most of the talks about sexuality are complete and at this age we are lovingly and gently re-enforcing everything we have been covering for the past 11 years. We may need to offer a few new insights and reminders, but always in a loving way. If that isn't the case with your parenting, it's certainly not too late!

If You Haven't Talked About Sexuality and Your Child is Now 13 or Older

First, make sure you have no shame about your own body, and understand that you're a temple of the Holy Spirit. After that's established, you'll need to get involved in your child's life: what do they like to do? Play sports? Piano? Poetry? We can use any positive thing they like to do to get into their world! You need to build rapport with them before you talk about sexuality.

• Also, pray for them and for the Holy Spirit to bless your talks with them. Once a comfortable rapport is built through time and activity and you understand them a little better, ask your teen out to the mall or a place to eat. Dating our teenagers is critical! Stay involved in their lives and get to know the parents and families of their friends.

• When you take them out to eat, start the conversation with something like, "I love you, and I enjoy being your parent." Then, ask them about the best part of their day and any hard parts of their day (questions that we should ask our teens every day). Then let your teen know that you've been praying for them! Let them know that you see them as a son or daughter of God and you really believe that God has blessed us by making our bodies "temples of the Holy Spirit." Then, ask them what they think about sexuality. Listen to what they say.

• If they don't talk, this can be understandable; you may need to have another Catholic parent (the same gender as your teen-aged child) spend some time with your teen so that they can teach them about a Catholic approach to sexuality. This can be very helpful in starting the conversation. Even if your teen does talk to you about sexuality, it's still important to have other Catholic parents in our lives whom we trust and who are willing to talk with our teens.

A Catholic Approach to Dating During the Teen Years

• During the adolescent years, hormones are raging, and teens don't yet have an adult brain because the prefrontal cortex is not fully formed. Guess what is the job of the prefrontal cortex? Yep, it's to control emotional urges from the body, and it's not fully formed until about age 24, and possibly later if there is heavy caffeine, drug, or alcohol use.

• Because of this biological fact, parents need to be their children's "external" prefrontal cortex. So it doesn't seem very logical to put a male and female teen together for the night and tell them to "have fun." Ideally, Catholic dating should happen later in life. This is easier to teach if you started doing so when they are at a younger, more impressionable age.

• This doesn't mean that teens can't have safe fun together, such as church lock-ins, groups going out with a trusted parent, having them over to your house so you know where they are and what they're doing, and spending time with other loving adults. When Jim was a teen he and his friends sometimes went to their teacher's house and played board games and they loved it! They valued the fact that other loving adults cared for them and wanted to spend time with them. We can only imagine that his parents loved it, too. Maureen's experience was different: living in a large urban area without a "tight" community, it was difficult to find other adults to host friend groups with similar values. Instead, Maureen spent most of her time in extracurricular activities and at a part-time job. Because she has always felt there was something of a vacuum in her teen experience, we're working hard to provide these experiences of camaraderie and social connection for our own teen-aged daughters.

We need to have other Catholic adults as our allies who will support what we have been teaching them all along about the beauty and goodness of our bodies. This is so important, especially when our teens want some normal space from parents, so we know where they are and who's teaching them.

Before You Continue

These questions aren't meant to be shame-based, but to examine habits.

1) Who taught you about sexuality? Was it positive? If it wasn't positive, what can you change when you teach your children about this beautiful gift?

2) Are you comfortable with your own sexuality? Why or why not?

3) What does Galatians 4:7 ("You are no longer a slave but a child, and if a child then also an heir, through God") mean to your sexuality?

4) Have you talked to your children yet about sexuality? If not, what tips from this chapter can you use to help with those little talks?

Prayer About Not Buying Society's Lies

All good and loving God, Your Word tells us that we are beautifully and wonderfully made. Our sexuality is an ineffable gift. Help me to navigate positively the many lies in our society that tell us otherwise. Send Your Spirit today so that my parenting will be empowered to focus on Jesus, who is our way, our truth, and our life. I pray this in the power of Your Holy Spirit and through Christ, our Lord. Amen.

Ninth Daily Dozen: Limit Unproductive Screentime 9

"I will not set before my eyes anything that is base." —Psalm 101:3

It probably isn't a big shocker that the *Daily Dozen of Catholic Parenting* would maintain that we as parents need to limit unproductive screentime. But we had to include it based on the sad news that we continue to hear about the excessive amounts of time our children spend watching a screen. Apparently, it's starting much earlier.

According to the *Archives of Pediatrics and Adolescent Medicine*, 40% of three-month-olds regularly watch television, DVDs, or videos. This is alarming, especially since nearly all experts agree that there should be no screentime for any child under two years of age. We need to get the word out about this ASAP.

We're also keenly aware that we have referenced various websites throughout this workbook. This is why we say "unproductive" screentime. Jim is smart-phone dependent and has been for years (Maureen, not so much—but she's learning!). We're okay with that because it's a tool that organizes his time and contains his Bible, the daily Mass readings, a concordance, and notes for talks and workbooks. It helps him as he seeks to be a good steward of the time God has granted him. However, if either of us were sitting in front of the phone for hours, that wouldn't be OK. There's a difference between productive screentime and unproductive screentime. The latter is mostly about sitting on the couch and channel surfing, or sitting in front of your electronic device, cell phone, or computer and net surfing with no direct, productive reason. This applies to our children and to us as parents. We all need to be aware of the pitfalls of unnecessary screentime.

Jim has worked with many clients who say they need their "downtime." He agrees with them and asks what they do for this downtime. The answer most of the time is . . . you guessed it, "watch TV or surf the net." This unproductive screentime really isn't downtime, according to the way God made our brain.

We All Need Downtime . . . But What is True Downtime?

". . . I am fearfully and wonderfully made," proclaimed the psalmist thousands of years ago (Psalm 139:14).

Wow, is that Psalm ever correct. God made the brain one big chemical and electrical factory . . . it's amazing. There are about 100 billion cells called neurons that compose this masterpiece, and they never touch each other! They communicate with each other via a complex web of electrical impulses and neurotransmitters (chemicals). The brain offers many paradoxes; we'll focus on the present issue of "downtime."

The brain is most at rest when it's active. It's during Rapid Eye Movement (REM) sleep that the brain is very active. The brain is so active during REM sleep that the body is literally paralyzed so that it can't act on the REM dreams. It's also during the deep sleep stages that the brain actually regenerates and rejuvenates itself. The brain is most restful and recreational while it's most active. If we could apply this bio-chemical truth in our parenting and families it could create more time for us to transform our families into the domestic churches that God desires. Yes, we need downtime and recreational time. But not in the form of watching most of what's on TV, or surfing most web pages because these can be, for the most part, passive and very unproductive activities at best.

At its worst, this screentime can be death dealing and can be a trap to allure us into "soft porn" (we hate that phrase because lust is lust) or gambling, or spending too much money, or just about any other enslavement that excessive and unproductive screentime can bring. Can you think of something more passive than watching TV? We can't. It's totally numbing, and that's why it's not true "downtime" or true recreational activity because, again, the brain is most at rest when it's active. In order to have true downtime we would need to do something that engages the brain.

If screentime isn't recreational, then what is?

We need silence, meditation, beauty, art, music, prayer, conversation (especially with our loved ones), nature, journaling, exercising, gardening, sewing, martial arts, creating scrapbooks (one of Maureen's favorites), teaching, reading, writing, singing (we both like this one), painting, and more. All of these activities are very much re-creational and can eventually replace any unproductive screentime.

When this biological truth was explained to us, it slowly began to change the way we viewed our own downtime. As a Gen-X-er Jim was raised with the beginning of video games (remember the old Atari), infant computers (nothing like we have now), and nearly unlimited TV time. Likewise, Maureen remembers spending a lot of time in front of the TV (particularly in the summer), although her parents tried to limit TV-time to two hours per day. We both considered TV/computer time as our downtime and time to "relax." When we learned about the biology of the brain and the paradoxes it offers, it really opened our eyes to see how mind-numbing TV and unproductive screentime can be. Fundamentally, this insight has changed most aspects of our life, including our parenting.

So now we ask you: do you or your children have difficulty with unproductive screentime? If so, let's review some realistic steps that will help you or your children stop this cycle.

Realistic Steps to Reduce Unproductive Screentime

What works for many people is to keep track of how much time they spend on unproductive screentime, which is called a "baseline."

Then, slowly start changing that behavior by adopting two behaviors that are equally important:

1) Reinvesting some of that time into more productive recreational time, such as a hobby, talking with loved ones, reading the Bible, and praying.

2) Trying to use the rest of the unproductive screentime a bit more productively. This might include buying a treadmill, exercise bike, free weights, or doing pushups and sit-ups while you watch TV. This could turn some unproductive screentime into time used for exercise, which we need anyway. If this applies to you, take time to complete the following questions to determine a baseline and try to figure out what you can do with that baseline.

"I use about_____ minutes of unproductive screentime per day." Have a loved one (spouse, accountable friend or mentor) review that to make sure it's accurate, because we all have a strong tendency to underestimate this time. Now determine a reduction percentage that will work for you.

For example, if your baseline is 120 minutes (two hours) of unproductive screentime per day and you think you can start by reducing that time by 50 percent, then you would start today by watching 60 fewer minutes of unproductive screentime. With that extra hour you could talk with your spouse or children, play a game with your children, pick up a hobby that you've wanted to learn, take a nap, exercise, etc.

What will you do with your extra time?

Now we need to address the screentime you have remaining. In our example above that would be about 60 minutes of unproductive screentime per day. With this hour of watching TV we would challenge you to exercise during it. Don't have a treadmill or bike? Can't afford one? That's OK. You can still do slow push-ups and sit-ups because those are free. You can jump rope, run in place, do jumping jacks, etc. There are many free options to do something productive while you watch TV. Keep this up for about three to four weeks and then see if you can start all over again with a new baseline in about a month (in our example, that new baseline will be an hour).

With this method, in a few short months you'll be free of unproductive screentime and, believe us, you won't miss it. That doesn't mean you'll stop screentime entirely, but it means you'll be "*unproductive* screentime-free." Again, there's a difference between unproductive and productive screentime. Next you'll want to do it for your children.

Note that you start this process first because once you're better at controlling unproductive screentime, you can teach your children to do the same. You will thank God for the freedom that you have. You'll also notice just how toxic our "entertainment" is, with the misuse of sexuality and emphasis on consumption and violence. You'll be free from all that, and your relationships can take on new life.

Maybe you don't have much unproductive screentime in your life, but your children probably do. If so, you can use a similar model to gradually address that. First, figure a baseline of unproductive screentime for each of your children. For example, maybe you have a child who watches two hours a day. Next, figure out a realistic percentage that you will use to slowly cut into that time and create other habits in their life. Start slowly, maybe with 20 minutes less each day. When you try to change your children's screentime you might also want to reward them for less screentime.

For example, let them know they can earn rewards for cutting back 20 minutes per day. Possible rewards could be small amounts of money, books, privileges, etc. By cutting that time in small percentages and re-investing that time into reading, relationships, playing outside, using their imagination, etc., you're teaching them a realistic model of cutting unproductive screentime. Set up a daily or weekly calendar and reward them weekly for their efforts. This will help teach them to use their screentime wisely as well. Depending on the baseline, eventually they will be at a level where you want them to be, and we think you'll notice other benefits as well.

That's exactly what happened to Bill and Jane, their marriage, and their family. Plus, they had another (very typical) side effect: an improved sex life! Here's their story.

Real Clinical Example of Benefits of Reduced Screentime

Bill is a professional and a business owner. He and his wife Jane are also busy parents. Bill works a lot and used to defend his "downtime" of TV watching. After Jim shared with him what we shared with you in this section about real downtime, Bill started to look at this habit and began to reinvest time into his marriage and family. In the session after Bill made these changes, Jane commented on how wonderful things had been going. Bill was cooking, playing with their child, and talking with her more often, all because he reinvested some time from watching TV into the relationship. Bill commented on their improved sex life as well, because Jane felt loved again. Bill still watches some TV, but now he's monitoring what he watches. And Jim is convinced that when he continues to see the fruit of re-investing screentime into relationship time (with our God, our loved ones, and ourselves), Bill will eventually build on these victories. Both Bill and Jane agreed that this has helped their marriage tremendously.

A Major Objection

One objection that we hear time and time again to this unproductive screentime is "I have to watch the world nightly news." We like to tell people that this really isn't "world" news. We both learned that when living in Jerusalem. If you really want to watch world news, try the BBC online, or www.worldmag.com for a Christian perspective, or their app. You'll be choosing to see less violent images than the standard TV news reports show while getting a more global perspective. And if you really want to be radical, try turning off your TV completely. Trust us: if the Martians land, someone will be sure to let you know!

A Few Words About Social Media

As a pastoral minister, Maureen frequently worked with couples and families who were preparing for the Sacraments of Marriage, Baptism, Eucharist, and Reconciliation, as well as families who were new to the parish. She would use the opportunity to encourage them to participate in parish life on a regular basis, particularly by coming to weekly Mass. Often one or more of them would object, "But we're so busy with work, kids' activities, and family that it's hard to find the time." Maureen would reply, "Can I ask you how much time you spend on Facebook each day?" This would almost always result in a look of embarrassment. Not that the point was to embarrass anyone but rather to invite people to consider that we make time for what we value.

And regarding value, our opinion about Facebook and other social media is that the cost/benefit ratio is pretty unfavorable. Yes, these media can be used to keep in touch with distant relatives and friends in our fast-paced world, but if we're honest, they can also be a vehicle for bragging, unhealthy comparisons with others (the old "Keeping Up with the Joneses"), and, in their most damaging form, marital infidelity. Some estimates say that one in five divorces is rooted in Facebook involvement (Jim has certainly witnessed this in counseling).

A further consequence of attachment to screens, whether computers, TV's, smartphones, tablets, or other devices, is that they can seriously impair our ability or willingness to be present to those around us. Who among us hasn't witnessed the bizarre scene in a restaurant or other public place, where people sitting at a table are more engaged with their hand-held screens than with each other?

As Catholic writers, speakers, parents and parishioners, we are acutely concerned that this reliance on screens inhibits our ability to be truly present to the living, breathing humans in our midst. It bears mentioning that as Catholics, for whom the Real Presence of Jesus in the Eucharist is a central belief and the "source and summit" of our lives (*Lumen Gentium*, 11), we simply must be truly present to our families, friends, and coworkers if we are ever to appreciate the Real Presence of Christ in the Eucharist. Indeed, in partaking of the Eucharist, we are called to be the presence of Christ to our world. It is worth praying and thinking about.

It is true that we live in a world dominated by social media and that our children are growing up in this world. Our job as parents is to help them navigate it. Suggesting or requiring that they totally unplug is probably impractical (although we do admire parents who hold off on letting their teens have their own phones until later in adolescence—or not at all). The question becomes: how are we instilling our values in a way that helps our children live by them, even in a media-saturated culture?

Before You Continue

1) What are your thoughts on the way the brain offers us a paradox about true downtime?

2) Do you or your children need new boundaries around screentime? If so, what is your plan to do this?

3) What are some of your favorite recreational activities?

4) What is your experience of Facebook and/or other social media? Do you find that it enhances your life? Is it a source of stress?

Ages & Stages: Media Use

All media are tools that must be used for the good of all and respect the dignity of each human being (violent media, pornography, etc. are clear violations of this principle). Here are some guidelines for children of different ages and stages that can help us become better Catholic parents in our digital age.

Birth to age 2

Absolutely no screentime at all for these tender, developing brains. The human brain begins developing about three weeks after conception, and during the first months of life outside the womb, the brain is making literally trillions of connections. Consider the study done by Dimitri Christakis, et. al. of the University of Washington's School of Medicine. It showed that for every hour of daily TV that kids watched from ages one to three, their risk for attention problems increased by 10 percent when they were seven years old (*Pediatrics* 113, no. 4. (2004) 708-715). Please spread the word that there should be no screentime for this age group!

What's needed during this time of development:

• Pray with your children daily; start this habit early and they will expect it as they grow older. Bless your children every day as well. Read books to them daily.

• Face-to-face time is needed (not digital but real physical face-to-face time). Babies respond to bold colors, lines, and shapes, as well as reading books, reading books, and reading more books. Avoid the temptation to use any electronic device during these years as a "baby-sitter" even for a short time. Put your child in an "exer-saucer" when you need to take a shower or a break.

• No TVs or screen in any bedrooms. Start this healthy habit early.

• Sing Christian lullabies to them and/or fun Christian songs (Twila Paris, Michael Card, Wee Sing, VeggieTales, etc.). Children love music.

• If you have a child in this age range and you have allowed some screentime, please consider stopping it. The child may throw a fit at first, but it will be short lived if it's replaced with loving relationship time.

Ages 3-4 years

The American Academy of Pediatrics suggests that kids in this age group spend no more than two hours a day total on all screentime (TV, videos, iPads . . . anything with a screen). Consider a 2006 study, which showed that preschoolers exposed to more than two hours of TV per day were three times more likely to be overweight (*Talking Back to Facebook* by James Steyer, pg. 109).

What's needed during this time of development:

• Pray with your children daily, read a children's Bible to them every night and bless them. The earlier these rituals are started, the better they take hold.

• Read daily to your child for at least 20 minutes, especially before bed. This can create a sense of calm in them.

• There are some excellent PBS shows, educational shows, or educational apps available for this age. Be very selective about them and remember to keep total screentime to less than two hours a day. As a constant and general rule, parents should be aware of what their children are watching on TV and what they're listening to on the radio. Don't assume that the content is appropriate for them simply because they are billed as a child's show. Many cartoons and sitcoms feature adults who are portrayed as clueless and not worthy of respect. Likewise, secular radio often contains lyrics that are in direct conflict with the Catholic values we are trying to teach our children. At the very least, be open to talking with your children about these shows and songs. Try to help them see what behaviors and attitudes are in keeping with our Catholic faith, and which are not.

• Sing Christian lullabies to them and/or fun Christian songs (Go Fish, Michael Card, CatChat, Wee Sing, etc.).

• No TV or screens in the bedroom! Start this early and be consistent.

• Remember that research shows that preschoolers are more easily influenced by ads than are older kids (*Archives of Pediatrics & Adolescent Medicine* 164, no. 5 (2010): 425 – 31). Keep this age group away from ads; be vigilant.

Ages 5-6

Studies suggest that children in this age group who spend more than two hours of screentime per day have an increased chance for attention, learning, and behavior problems. That same research shows that children this age who are exposed to violence are more likely to behave aggressively toward others (Amanda Gardener, "Kids' TV Time Linked to School Woes, Bad Habits," Health.com, May 3, 2010).

What's needed during this time of development:

• Pray with your children daily, read a children's Bible to them every night and bless them. The earlier these rituals are started, the better they take hold. Children this age love to be blessed and prayed over. Tell them daily that they are children of God.

• Have specific rules for Internet usage (e.g., if your 5-year old wants to surf the web, surf with them).

• Christian music is a huge blessing at this age: Go Fish, Wee Sing, CatChat and Vacation Bible School (VBS) material can be very helpful in teaching them the faith.

• As with any age, our children learn from us! We need to set good digital boundaries for ourselves, and they will follow. How many hours of non-work related time do we as parents spend in front of a screen? No shame, but it's a critical question. Many digital attitudes are caught; not taught.

• NO screens in their bedrooms, including systems such as gaming devices. Please pray and think about taking them out now; you'll be happy about this decision when your child is a teen.

Ages 7-8

TV is the main media attraction for children this age, according to Aviva Lucas Gutnick et al, ("Always Connected: The New Digital Media Habits of Young Children," March 2011). It's sad, but more than half of 7-to 8-year-olds have TVs in their bedrooms (Johns Hopkins University and the CDC, March 2007). This is not good for many reasons! A 2009 study at Yale University revealed that kids ages seven to 11 who watched a 30-minute cartoon with food commercials ate 45% more snacks while watching, compared to kids who watched a cartoon without commercials.

What's needed during this time of development:

• Pray with your 7- and 8-year olds every day, and read to them. Christian music is great at this age. Imagination is growing, so have them paint, color, create a story, or do any other artistic endeavor; it can be as simple as coloring rocks outside.

• Kids this age are still very compliant to parents, so we must limit their screentime to 1.5–2 hours a day maximum. If parents set this limit, they will follow. They may buck it in the beginning, but it's better to do this now before they're tweens. Parents are still the strongest influence on their children at this age, so be a good example and teach prudent use of screentime.

• If your child has a TV in their room, please take it out now. Numerous studies show that this is not good because they will just watch more TV. Simply explain to your children that you love them and just like you try to give them good food for their bodies, you also want to give them good food for their minds and souls. Then take out the TV. They may complain in the beginning but it will be so worth it.

• At this age make sure to use all parental settings on your browsers and pray about using a safety net like "net-nanny" (realizing that even this isn't 100% effective). Teach your children to never erase their browser history; if they do, you won't know what sites they're visiting. Consider establishing a consequence if they erase their history.

Ages 9-10

According to the Kaiser Family Foundation (January, 2010) 90% of children in this age group are playing online games. Some can be innocent (Webkinz, Club Penguin, etc.), but we would still invite parents to check out their content independently and then play them with your children within specific time limits. For example, our children had a Webkinz account, so Jim got one as well and played online with them. Children are vulnerable, so it makes sense to be vigilant about what they're watching. For example, a 2010 study from the American Academy of Pediatrics found that 75% of all prime time shows contain sexual content but rarely show the risks of sexual behavior. Consider the 2010 study published in *Scientific American* (January 25, 2011) by Monica Heger, titled "Preteens and Glowing Screens." This study showed that the more time tweens spend in front of a screen, the more likely they would feel sad, negative, and lonely—no matter what the amount of their physical activity! We parents need to act!

What's needed during this time of development:

• Children need to feel more and more like they belong. Weekly church attendance and being involved in a weekly youth group will help. Daily prayer time and blessings from their parents are critical to giving them a deep sense of belonging to your family and to the family of God. Talk to them about cyber safety at age-appropriate levels.

• Researchers at UCLA found in 2011 that for kids ages 9 to 11, "fame" is now the number one trait they value. Since parents are still the number one influence on their children at this age, we must teach them the truth that fame is not the goal of our Christian identity; building the Kingdom of God is. This starts at home by parents shutting off highly influential screen content and spending time with our kids by going for walks, bike rides, praying together, reading together, etc.

• We recommend no cell phones yet. Cell phones can be helpful, but most tweens don't need them. Introduce cell phones when they're a help to the parents. We suggest that as a parent, you establish the right (and even the expectation) to review anything on your child's cell phone (text messages, sites visited, etc.) This is not an invasion of their privacy; rather, it is you exercising your responsibility as a parent and guardian of your child's well-being.

• Make sure all of your digital boundaries are clearly set now, so that they can continue to work smoothly into the tween and teen years. For example, screentime is only used when exercise and homework are done. No screens in their bedrooms. Be a good role model.

Ages 11-12

Inform your children they won't have an "adult" brain until they're about 24 years old. According to Nielsen, children ages 9–12 with smart phones send about 1,146 texts per month! This should count as part of their two hour max screentime per day. A survey conducted by the American Academy of Pediatrics asked 1,560 youth ages 10-17 if they had received nude or nearly nude images of others. They found that 7.1% had received such images . . . that's over 100 tweens and teens who have received nude images.

What's needed during this time of development:

• Pray for and with your children daily. Tweens are open to prayer and direction from their parents, so we need to utilize this open window, because it can close when they become teens.

• If you have not talked to your tweens about the beauty of the human body and human sexuality, please do so. God made our bodies and they are good. The gift of sexuality is so good that we as Christians believe we need to leave it wrapped up until marriage. Tweens are naturally interested in sexuality, so talk openly about it with an emphasis on the Christian understanding of the goodness of the gift of sexuality.

• Parents are the number one influence on tweens and teens. We can cancel cable TV (one of the best decisions we made for our marriage and family). We can teach our children to use technology and not be used by it. See the note under "Ages 3-4" about parental oversight of TV and radio content.

• If you don't already have other Catholic adults in your lives who can be influential in the lives of your children and with whom you get together frequently as families, pray about this opportunity. These Catholic allies may be critical when your children become teens and want more time away from the family. If that happens, send them to the approved families that you already know: families who share your digital boundaries and Christian values. Your parish is a good place to connect with other Catholic families.

• We recommend no Facebook for tweens—we don't care how much they cry about it. We don't even think Facebook should be an option for 14 or 15 year olds. It's reasonable to consider letting our kids have an account when they've proven to their parents that they're responsible enough to drive a vehicle. If they have an account, make sure you can monitor it and "friend" them.

Ages 13-15

Inform or remind your children that they won't have an "adult" brain until they're about 23 or 24, when the prefrontal cortex (PFC) is fully formed (longer if there is chemical/screentime addiction). Inform or remind your teen that the PFC is the part of the brain that stops us humans from acting on our emotional impulses. It's critically important to teach every parent and every teen about this!

• Consider a recent study that shows kids up to age 18 who spend more time with screens have lower grades and less contentment compared to other kids ("Media in the Lives of 8-18 Year Olds," Kaiser Family Foundation, January 2010). Our teens still look to us as the number one influence in their lives, so we need to be highly aware of our own media consumption habits and lead by example.

• Sadly, according to a poll at teenangels.org, roughly 20% of the teen girls said they had taken a sexually provocative, nude, or explicit cell selfie and shared it with others, most often their boyfriends. 14% of the boys shared the "private" images with others when they broke up with their girlfriends. And 44% of the boys polled admitted to having seen at least one of these sexual images of a classmate.

What's needed during this time of development:

• If you haven't started a routine of praying together as a family, please do so. This can be a grounding time for teens and adults.

• Share at least four meals per week as a family with no media (no phones, no cell phones, iPads, iPods, TV, etc.). Try talking about the best part of each family member's day, the hardest part, and what he/she learned that day. Incidentally, breakfast counts as a meal if you're all together.

• Keep talking about Internet safety, sexting, cyberbullying, and boundaries.

• Teens often want to pull away from their family of origin, which can be very normal. Church youth groups are essential during this time, and you may have to call upon the other Catholic parents whom your teen likes to help shape and direct your teen. It takes the whole Body of Christ to form and raise children.

• Puberty can be a confusing time of life. Normalize those feelings but also talk about how the teen years can be a huge blessing to the world and to the teen going through it. Teens have an energy and optimism that needs to be tapped into and harnessed by the adults who love them.

Ages 16-18

Consider some facts from the Kaiser Family Foundation:

• Kids and teens ages 8-18 spend nearly 4 hours a day in front of a TV screen and almost 2 additional hours on the computer (outside of schoolwork) and playing video games.

• Counting all media outlets, 8-18 year-olds devote an average of 7 hours and 38 minutes to using entertainment media across a typical day.

• By now you're well aware of the dangers that too much screentime can bring to kids of every age, but especially to our 16–18 year olds. This is the time of life when they can be using their teen energy for volunteering, mastering a second or third language, figuring out which college to attend and where God is calling them to be with their unique gifts.

• If they're spending the average of almost 8 hours a day on screen usage, many of the positive aspects of this age and stage will be lost. We need to be the parent during these years and say "no" to most violent movies and/or video games. The Lord desires that we lead by example, so we need to ask ourselves how much non-work screentime we ingest on a daily basis. Older teens still want us to lead.

• Youth in this age group don't want to be in control! They want to have a voice, but they don't want to be in control, because it stresses them out. They want to know that they can be a "kid." If you need to, set up a realistic plan to cut down screentime by 10-15% each week, track your time and celebrate your victories. It takes about 60 days to develop a new habit, so make sure you give yourself enough time to achieve success.

What's needed during this time of development:

• Family prayer time and church prayer time is critical during these years. It helps our older teens to know that life is not all about them. It helps ground them. Youth group can give them a safe place to play and pray together and be a teen. ·

• Play with your older teen: take them on in an appropriate video game, or watch a movie together and talk about the themes. Some great choices are "The Grace Card," "Courageous," "Fireproof," "Facing the Giants," and "Soul Surfer." There are many decent Christian movies available. We need to watch them with our teens and use them as discussion tools. Continue talking about cyber safety.

• During these later teen years, it's critical to have trusted Catholic adults in your lives so when our 16–18 year olds want to naturally separate from us, we can offer them safe, loving adults and families to spend time with. It takes loving adults willing to say, "I will be the family that your older teen can go to when they want some space from you."

• If possible, establish your home as a house for kids to play board games, some appropriate video sports games, ping-pong, air hockey, dartboards, or other types of teen activities. That way you know where your son or daughter will be and they can have friends over to have fun with your family.

Prayer About Unproductive Screentime

Almighty God, I am created in Your image and likeness and I thank You for this gift. Help me to name and tame the negative images that bombard me daily and are contrary to Your love. Send Your Spirit into our family today so that we can be honest with ourselves about what true "downtime" is. Empower us to use our time wisely and so cooperate with Your loving plan. We pray this in the power of the Holy Spirit and through Christ our Lord. Amen.

Helpful Resources and Websites for Digital Holiness

Some are not Christian, but they can be very helpful.

• https://dns.norton.com/configureRouter.html. Anyone can use this to configure a home router using Norton's filtered IP address. This service is free, there's nothing to download, and it protects every device connected to your home router! If the above site doesn't work, search for "configure my router with Norton."

• www.covenanteyes.com: Excellent monitoring software for the whole family.

• www.family.org: Dr. James Dobson's website.

• www.aacc.net: The American Association of Christian Counselors.

• www.ncpc.org: The National Crime Prevention Council. Click on "Internet safety."

• www.cyberbullying.us: A very informational site with research and resources for parents, teens, and others.

• www.stopcyberbullying.org: Full of legal information.

• www.wiredsafety.com: Full of helpful information on Internet safety.

• www.teenangels.org: A great site where teens, tweens, parents, and others can learn how to be safer online.

• www.drdavewalsh.com: The site of Mind Positive Parenting founder Dr. David Walsh, who's an expert in parenting, family, and the effects of media on young people. This site contains many of his lectures and blogs.

10

Tenth Daily Dozen:
Laugh Often and Teach Optimism

"Then our mouth was filled with laughter and our tongue with shouts of joy."
—Psalm 126:2

This Psalm pretty much sums it up, right? We want to celebrate all that God is doing in our lives, and that celebration truly includes laughter. Even when times are hard, God continues to promise the hope of resurrection laughter from all the deaths we go through.

In 2004 our youngest child was born with Down syndrome and severe pulmonary hypertension (high blood pressure in the lungs). Shortly after his birth a team had to air-lift him to Children's Hospital in Minneapolis, Minnesota, where the specialists and nurses did a wonderful job caring for him. There is nothing funny about that story. But, again, God brings resurrection from all deaths in our lives.

Now David is growing and doing well. He has taught us the gift of laughter all over again. He laughs at things that surprise and inspire us, and his laugh is infectious. When he was younger, his favorite breakfast was a peanut butter and honey sandwich. Nothing funny about that, either. But he loved the way one of us put on the honey. We'd put the bread on a plate, take the cap off the honey, and then say to him "Ready, set . . ." and David would say "O" (he couldn't say the "G" sound). Then we'd raise the honey container up in the air (sometimes above his head), as honey came streaming out. David would laugh enthusiastically as the honey dripped down on the bread in a circle, and sometimes on the table. What a gift he is in our lives and in the Body of Christ!

As parents we all have these funny stories about our children. In fact it would be good to start a website just devoted to that; we could call it whenkidslaugh.com. Laughter is so needed in our lives, and children instinctively know how to do it. Do you know that when we laugh our brain releases good chemicals called "endorphins"? That is a word that literally means "internal morphine." What a deal! When we laugh out loud our brain actually releases a chemical that is similar to morphine, and those effects can hang out in the brain for about 12 to 24 hours! So laugh, laugh, and laugh some more; even at yourself (appropriately).

Laughing at ourselves can be tricky at first. Sometimes it requires letting go of the unrealistic expectations we hold of ourselves and our family members. One story that Maureen has found helpful in this regard comes from Dr. Janet E. Smith, the professor of moral theology who champions the Church's teaching on sexuality and the goodness of marriage and children. In one of her talks, Dr. Smith relates a conversation she had with a mom of 17 children. Dr. Smith was invited to spend the day at their home, and after a few hours she asked the mother, "How do you keep track of everyone and get everything done?" The mom's reply: "We say 'Oh well' a lot!"

This ability to "go with the flow" and to laugh at certain situations is practically a survival technique in family life. We both credit our spiritual directors with the patience and wisdom needed for teaching us this valuable lesson in life. When we are able to appropriately laugh at our own quirks, we can slowly become less self-conscious and more God-conscious. Then, the prayer of John the Baptist becomes our prayer: "He must increase, but I must decrease" (Jn 3:30).

This life that we live isn't just about us: it is about Jesus Christ. We exert way too much energy being too serious and we need to learn to laugh. But as we learn how to laugh we also need to use laughter wisely as well. Laughter is powerful, especially if it is not used properly.

Real Clinical Example About Inappropriate Laughter

Jim remembers Chuck and Nancy and how they had to learn to use appropriate laughter. They had been married for over 30 years. They had raised their family and were now finding marriage a chore. In fact, they were even thinking about divorce as some couples do at this stage in life. Chuck complained because he wasn't getting enough sexual intimacy, and Nancy complained because she wasn't feeling loved.

When Jim examined their marital dynamics closely, he found that Chuck was treating Nancy like one of the guys with his sarcastic "humor." We place humor in quotes here because nothing about sarcasm is funny. As we mentioned in Chapter 5, sarcasm is from the Greek word "sarx," meaning "flesh." A possible transliteration could read "to tear or rip the flesh away." That's what we do when we use sarcasm. We rip the flesh off of the body of the relationship in which we use it, and that's never funny.

When this was uncovered in their marriage, Jim invited Chuck to continue being funny (he was truly funny; Nancy loved that and so did Jim) but to stop the sarcasm. His reply was memorable: "Jim, that will kill me; that is who I am."

What do you think Jim told him? (hint: re-read the first Daily Dozen). Yes, he told him of his true identity as a son of God. Chuck believed that he needed to be sarcastic in order to fit into his family of origin. He listened to the wound instead of to the Word. That's a trap many of us fall into. Jim told him he wasn't born talking sarcastically and that it was a learned behavior. He also encouraged him to start telling himself that he is a son of God and to expect the behavior of sarcasm to change as he starts acting more and more from his identity as a son of God. Chuck agreed that it was worth a shot. It took a few sessions, but he did stop the sarcasm; it seems he surprised himself and his wife. When they discussed sexuality in their relationship, Nancy said that because Chuck wasn't using the sarcasm, she was feeling more loved. And as a natural by-product, they were sharing more sexual intimacy.

Fostering Optimism

While fostering a good, holy sense of humor (without sarcasm) is very important in our Christian parenting, we also need to teach our children how to be optimistic and happy. Yes, you read that right. We need to literally coach our children into being optimists. If you're reading this and thinking that would be impossible because you're a pessimist, you're absolutely correct. A pessimist could not coach a child into becoming a happy optimist. What we tell parents in that situation is that you need to become an optimist first, and then hand on this wonderful, life-giving, game-changing gift of optimism and happiness to your children.

How do you become an optimist? For starters, go back to the first chapter of this book and focus completely on your great identity—you are a child of God, and God is an optimist.

It is God who can turn our sorrow into happiness, and He has already done that through the life, death, and resurrection of Jesus. Jesus in turn sends us His Holy Spirit, the spirit of joy and happiness. We want to teach ourselves and our children to be optimistic and happy because God desires this.

Only an optimist could redeem an entire, unfaithful, ungrateful people through His only begotten Son, Jesus Christ. Because Abba is an optimist, we ought to be as well. And, after learning it ourselves, we want to teach it to our children. It may be true that some of our children are more pessimistic by nature, but we need to recognize that our children's identity in Christ is far more powerful than their personality traits (you may need to re-read the second chapter of this book, which discusses this truth). While it may be more challenging with children who are more negative, don't give up! This is critically important work!

There are multiple studies that prove that being more optimistic and happy is good for your mind, body, soul and relationships. Here are just a few of these studies. And if you want more, simply Google "optimism and health" and you'll quickly see what we mean.

After the horrific attacks of 9-11-2001, many of the survivors developed Post-Traumatic Stress Disorder (PTSD), but not all did. Dr. Barbara Fredrickson found that people whose happiness levels were high before the attack did not develop PTSD, and those whose pre-attack levels of happiness were lower did worse compared to those who were happier and more optimistic. The unhappy people developed PTSD at a higher rate (Fredrickson, B.L, Tugade, M.M., Waugh, C.E. & Larkin, G.R. (2003). ("What good are positive emotions in crisis? A prospective study of resilience and emotion following the terrorist attacks on the United States on September 11, 2001." *Journal of Personality and Social Psychology*, 84, 365-376).

Moreover, studies show that optimism reduces heart attacks (Giltay, E. et al. (2006). ("Dispositional optimism and the Risk of Cardiovascular death, The Zutphen Elderly Study." *Archives of Internal Medicine,* 166,431-436.)

So how do we become more optimistic and happy? First, we recognize all that God has done for us and thank God daily for salvation. As parents, we are well positioned to understand the importance of gratefulness. Just think of your own children. How often have you gone out of your way to do something special or difficult for them, and their response has been lukewarm or worse? In order for them to be thankful, we have to teach them how. And in turn, we have to be mindful about being grateful to God.

We can and should be deliberate in telling God how grateful we are for His Son, Jesus Christ, and for their gift of the Holy Spirit to us. As Catholics we share in an incredibly rich heritage of grace; indeed the very word "eucharist" means "thanksgiving." We live most fully and joyfully when we are aware and appreciative of the great gifts we share as members of the Body of Christ. As we do this we begin to develop the fruits of the Holy Spirit, and "joy" is one of those powerful fruits we read about in Galatians.

We can also build on the natural strengths that God has given us and our children, and as we do that they become happier by using their natural gifts.

A powerful, free, secular tool is the "Values in Action" survey. It contains the largest database on character strengths, and it's free for adults and children. We recommend that parents take it first and then your children can take it as well. Visit: www.viacharacter.org to take the survey and see your top strengths.

Once you know the top strengths of yourself and your children, make sure that you do at least three things in the top category every day. This is a great way to build confidence, optimism, and joy in our families.

Another way to increase our own optimism or our children's optimism is through prayer. In the Gospel of Mark, Chapter 11, Jesus tells us that when we pray we are to believe we have received it, and it will be ours. We need to pray optimism, self-confidence, and joy into our lives and into the life of our children.

Real Clinical Example About Praying for Optimism

Jim invited a dad (we'll call him Tom) to pray over his daughter, Kelly, who had difficulties with self-love and self-acceptance. Jim taught Tom to pray this prayer over his daughter every night, while putting his hand on his daughter's head: "God, thank you that at Jesus' name every knee has to bend. The knees of our self-doubt and negativity have to bend. May your Holy Spirit bless Kelly with good self-love and self-acceptance. Thank you, God, that even now she has accepted herself as good and loves herself." The first night Tom prayed over his daughter, she actually shook her head "No" during this prayer, which saddened and surprised him. But with Jim's encouragement, Tom persisted, and gradually, Kelly no longer shook her head "no" during the phrase "thank you that even now she has accepted herself as good and loves herself." This is the lesson we learn from the Gospel of Mark when we pray self-love, self-acceptance, optimism, and happiness into existence over ourselves and our children.

These are very powerful realities and we ask every family to do them! We can teach our children optimistic skills through many different ways: One simple way is to ask them at dinner what was the one thing they were thankful for that day. Or, for those children who like to write, they can start a "thankful journal." For children who like to color or paint, they can make a picture of what they were thankful for that day. At night when praying with your family, always start the prayer by thanking God for Jesus and His Holy Spirit, then thank God for all your children and list them by name. This teaches our children to have a radar of appreciation in their lives.

Teaching our children to avoid drama as teens is a great way to help them become more optimistic because drama in school and in life drags everyone down.

Before You Continue

1) What role does laughter play in your family?

2) Do you as a parent need to grow in optimism before you teach it to your children?

3) What concepts in this chapter can help you become more optimistic? And, what ways can you pass this optimism and joy onto your children?

Prayer About Laughter and Optimism

All loving God, in wisdom You created laughter to brighten our days, and You share Your optimism with us so that we can build Your Kingdom. Help us to develop these tremendous gifts within our families. Send us Your Spirit to open up our tired relationships with the new life that hope and joy bring. We ask this in the name Jesus our Lord. Amen.

11

Eleventh Daily Dozen:
Becoming Parents and Families Who Serve

"For the Son of Man came not to be served but to serve." —Mark 10:45

What a truth! Christ our Lord did not come to be served, as He had been by angels from before time began, but to serve. The Second Person of the Trinity who always has been and always will be came to serve those He created! What a mind-boggling truth! Yet that is exactly what Christ did and in doing so left us the supreme model for parenting and family life.

There are two ways to serve in a family: "in-reach" and "outreach." The first is a type of serving that will allow the Holy Spirit to heal any hurts that need healing in our own families. In reality, the first 10 Daily Dozen are about "in-reach."

Outreach is a more advanced, yet critically important, aspect of family life. That is why this Daily Dozen appears later in this workbook, because we can only truly serve others after we have worked on any "in-reach" that needs to be done in our own families.

To illustrate, here is another clinical example:

Real Clinical Example About In-Reach Before Outreach

Bob and Mary went to see Jim for marriage counseling years ago. Their marriage was a mess! It lacked communication, affection, and trust. Mary's need for spending time together was not being met. In fact, not many of her needs were being met. When Jim asked the reasons for this, Bob said with an almost proud demeanor, "I spend much of my time with the youth group and doing church work."

Jim almost fell out of his chair at that response. When asked, Mary confirmed what Bob had said. Jim asked Bob if he really thought God would call him away from his wife and children consistently in order to volunteer. Eventually the real truth came out: Bob had a close female friend to whom he was "ministering" at church. Jim had no reason to believe that any physical or sexual boundaries were broken in this relationship, but there were emotional, temporal, and verbal boundaries that were broken, and these are very serious boundaries in a marriage. Bob didn't see this as Jim did, and he never returned to counseling. We hope he eventually came to the truth that before we do "outreach" we have to do "in-reach."

Ideally, God wants us to reach out when the time is right in our families, and that will wax and wane with our life. The Church needs to understand that, and most do. This whole workbook is full of in-reach ideas that we hope have been helpful. These ideas can help bring healing and resurrection to your family and will help you understand that God has good plans for your family. Here are a few more ideas that can prompt more solid in-reach in your family: Let your children know that we are called to serve each other in a family, based on Christ's life. This type of serving is not in a slave-like way, but rather in a way that shows our children what leadership is all about: submission to God's will. And as Romans 8:28 points out, that will is for the good. Finding a balance between serving our children and not being a slave to them can be a tough task. We like to use the word "team" to convey this balance. We frequently let our children know that we are all on the same team and that we need to work together.

For example, sometimes when there are dirty clothes on the floor, and they don't belong to you, you can point out to your children, " I am being a team player and picking up these clothes." Not to say "Hey, look at me!" Nor should you do this all the time because it isn't advisable to take away from their daily tasks. Rather, you can do this because we need to lead by example as parents. When we are able to serve each other as a family it empowers us to reach out to others. Family life was never meant to be just us under our roof. When our families are ready for it, the Lord desires that we do outreach to other people in our community as well.

Incidentally, our Catholic tradition is filled with examples of people living out their commitment to Christ by doing outreach and service. Many of them are formally acknowledged as saints, while others inspire us by their good deeds that still bear fruit today. Just two examples are the many women religious who founded and staffed the Catholic schools in our country, and the U.S. Bishops who founded Catholic Relief Services, which today gives assistance to 130 million people in 90 countries.

Remember the sobering message in the Letter of James (a challenging letter that is often ignored): "Do you want to be shown, you senseless person, that faith apart from works is barren?" (James 2:20). This is not exactly one of those feel-good verses that is preached on. Ideally, our works of love should flow from our faith and not from a sense of shame or duty. The earlier we begin with outreach, the better, as long as it is good for our family (remember Bob and Mary). By beginning early, our children will become used to serving those in our community and will accept that it is just something that we do because our Lord did it. Assuming that now is a good season for your family to do some outreach, the next page has ideas for how you and your family can build the Kingdom together.

Ideas for Outreach

- Recommit to the Catholic tradition of observing Friday as a day of abstinence from some food or activity (e.g. car radio, TV, soda, alcohol, etc.) and pray for a person in need.
- Serve a meal at the Salvation Army or work in the Catholic Charities food shelf.
- Sponsor a child through an international organization.
- Visit a local nursing home.
- Write your elected officials to enact passages of just laws.
- Teach faith formation at your parish, or take a Scripture class.
- Volunteer at the Boys and Girls Club.
- Sign up for a meal-packing session at Kids Fighting Hunger.
- Make meals for a Ronald McDonald House (we stayed there when David was ill and were moved to tears by the sense of warmth and hospitality.)
- Sign up to be part of your parish prayer chain.
- Call an elderly neighbor and help rake their leaves or mow their lawn.
- Limit spending on gifts and then donate the portion saved.
- Visit someone in the hospital. Feel free to add your own.

How about in your parenting and your family life? Take some time now to focus on how you serve.

Before You Continue

1) Do you have any major in-reaching work that needs to be done? If so, what would that be?

2) Have any of the ideas in this workbook helped with those in-reaching tasks? If so, which ones have been most beneficial?

3) Is now the right time for your family to regularly serve with outreach? If so, what activity holds appeal for your family?

4) If you are currently involved in outreach, what has been a meaningful experience of service for your family?

Prayer About Serving

All good and ever loving God, You sent Christ into our broken world to serve it and redeem it. He in turn sends His Spirit into my heart today so that I can follow his divine lead. Open up our relationships so that the love You have for us will empower us to show our love for each other in word and deed, starting with our family members. We ask this through Christ our Lord and in the power of the Holy Spirit. Amen.

12

Twelfth Daily Dozen:
Ask for Guidance When You Need It

"Without counsel, plans go wrong, but with many advisers they succeed."
—Proverbs 15:22

Jim once worked with John and Lisa on their parenting and their marriage. It took John a while to open up to the whole process of Christian counseling. He had seen and heard good things about our clinic and had even referred others to us, which is always a tremendous honor. Still, John was reluctant to enter into his own journey of healing. But he was faithful to the therapy and they made a little progress. After about a year into the therapy he said, "Jim, thanks for this help; it really does help, but I wish I could have figured this out on my own."

John had unwittingly pointed out the perpetual roadblock to any transformation: "I wish I could have figured this out on my own." Once Jim was able to discuss this with John and Lisa, their marriage and family did some major transforming. It was awesome to watch the Holy Spirit at work healing this marriage and healing their parenting! They received all this transformation because John got over that internal and nearly eternal unconscious "on my own" illusion.

We all hear that voice at times: "You don't need anyone else—figure it out yourself." Look at the rotten fruit of this attitude: a high divorce rate, children abusing their parents, and parents abusing their kids. We see the news with its pessimism (because good news doesn't sell), and we encounter daily obstacles that interfere with positive parenting.

Of course, even with the persuasiveness of doing all this "on my own" the good news is still the Good News, Jesus Christ our Lord. Christ told us that we need not fear because God has numbered even the hairs on our head (Luke 12:7). That's how much God loves you! God cares for you tenderly and calls you His own child. So when the difficulties come we need to remember that parenting alone is impossible: in fact, anything alone is impossible because we were created for relationship and we are never alone.

Christ made sure of that by sending the Spirit into our hearts and by incorporating us into His Body. 1 Cor. 12 teaches us that we are all members of the same Body, and that we all have a different role in that one Body. So when you need help, ask for it.

As parents, we have often needed help, and we thank God for the kind and faithful Catholics in our life who have graciously given us that help. Asking for help is not a sign of weakness. It does take some getting used to, as John discovered. But when you ask a trained and trustworthy person for help, you can prepare for the transforming love of God to pour in because God has good plans for you.

How to Find Help

First, contact your parish staff member (pastor, pastoral minister, parish nurse, parish secretary) who can give you a list of local Catholic therapists. The Diocesan Office of Marriage and Family Life is another resource. Also, many cities/dioceses have an office of Catholic Charities, which provides counseling on a sliding-fee scale. We also encourage you to request information from friends who have been assisted by a Catholic therapist, because often the best referrals are by word-of-mouth. And pray for the guidance of the Holy Spirit in leading you to a person who can help you, your spouse, and your family grow into the children God calls you to be.

Before You Continue

1) Do you need to ask for help in an area in your life?

2) Do you find it hard or easy to ask for help? Why?

Prayer About Asking for Help When Needed

Ever present God, You love me so tenderly and completely that You provide people in my life who will help me and my family. Please send Your Spirit into my heart that I may understand how good it is to ask for help. Heal any pride that may prevent me from acting on the truth that we are all members of the same Body of Christ. When I need help, empower me to ask for it. I pray this through Christ our Lord and in the power of the Holy Spirit. Amen.

Cut-out Reminder: I Am a Child of God

The following pages have a few cut-out reminders that may help your parenting. If you are going to use these reminders, we recommend that before you cut them out take some clear packing tape and do a "daddy lamination." Jim has been using that technique with arts and crafts for years as a part-time stay-at-home dad. Put clear packing tape over both sides of the reminder you want, and then cut it out. The packing tape will act as an inexpensive way to laminate the card and will make it last for years to come.

This is what we have on our bathroom mirrors:

I am a
child of *God.*
Treat me
lovingly.

I am a
child of *God.*
Treat me
lovingly.

I am a
child of *God.*
Treat me
lovingly.

I am a
child of *God.*
Treat me
lovingly.

Cut-Out Reminder: Scriptural Truths About Who I Am

Pray with and understand the following Scripture passages, because they can begin to heal your negative images of God. As your negative image of God heals, your parenting will start becoming more positive. Pray with these images and memorize them. Cut them out and display them where you will see them daily.

+ "We are children of God." (Romans 8:16)
+ "See what love the Father has given us, that we should be called children of God." (I John 3:1)
+ "Do not fear, for I have redeemed you; I have called you by name, you are mine." (Isaiah 43:1)
+ "No one shall be able to stand against you all the days of your life. As I was with Moses, so I will be with you; I will not fail you or forsake you." (Joshua 1:5)
+ "As a mother comforts her child, so will I comfort you." (Isaiah 66:13)
+ "Peace I leave with you; my peace I give to you . . . Do not let your hearts be troubled, and do not let them be afraid." (John 14:27)

Answers to SEEN

Answers to page 57: "SEEN"

S= Smiling Appropriately. Using appropriate smiles tells the other person that we are listening intently to them and that they can trust our relationship. Smiles create warmth in our conversation and allow the other person to see love.

E= Eye Contact. Regular eye contact can be warm and inviting. Staring can create discomfort, but gentle eye contact tells a person you care. Ideally, we should not talk to our children until we can see their eyes. It's tempting to raise your voice to talk to a child in a bedroom when you're in the kitchen. But when you consider the importance of this nonverbal mode of communication, it's a good reminder not to do that. Try to use eye contact so that your children can see good communication modeled to them.

E= Eyebrows. Believe it or not, when you raise your eyebrows it almost says "I am being sincere here; you can trust me to listen to you." It may sound a little weird, but if you have never tried this non-verbal, practice it in a mirror until it becomes more natural. This is an especially powerful action in communication. Try it today and see what happens.

N= Nodding Your Head. Not nodding like you're falling asleep and snoring, but nodding with intent shows the person that you are listening to them and following their train of thought.

*As you practice being **SEEN** today, may it bless your relationships with transformation and peace.*

About the Authors

Married since 1995, Jim and Maureen Otremba have both been stay-at-home parents (part-time) since 1999. They have three children in their home (ages 16, 14, and 11) and seven children in heaven.

Since 1996, Jim has worked with children, adults, families, and couples. He is the owner of the Center for Family Counseling, Inc., in St. Cloud, Minnesota, where he provides Christian counseling. (For more information visit www.healinginchrist.com). Jim holds a Master of Divinity degree from St. John's University (Collegeville, MN) and a Master's in Applied Psychology from St. Cloud State University. He is a Licensed Independent Clinical Social Worker in Minnesota and provides Catholic life-coaching through www.coachinginchrist.com.

Maureen holds a Master of Arts with a concentration in Scripture from St. John's University. She has served in faith formation, marriage preparation, university administration, and pastoral care and taught high school in both Catholic and public schools for 10 years.

Jim and Maureen are the primary authors of *Fully Engaged: Growing Toward Lasting Fidelity*, a Catholic catechetical premarital inventory and formation program for engaged couples (www.getfullyengaged.com). They have also developed *Banquet of Love: The Eucharist as Weekly Marriage Enrichment*, which provides marriage enrichment to Catholic couples in a retreat/workshop format, or through the program's companion DVD and workbook (www.eucharisticmarriage.com).

Jim and Maureen love to present workshops and have worked with married couples, deacons and their wives, parents, and other groups in Minnesota and around the nation. If your parish or diocese needs energetic, dynamic speakers, contact the Otrembas by email: jimotremba@gmail.com or maureenotremba@gmail.com. They would be honored to work with your needs.

May God bless you and your family.

What Others Have Said About the Otrembas' Material

". . . most practical and helpful in making immediate improvements within our marriage."

"Thank you for your ministry—I'll be watching for your book and waiting for additional seminars."

"I love learning concrete ways to deal with stress and anxiety."

"Every couple came away with an enriched understanding of the spiritual aspect of our married life."

"We really enjoyed the passion and enthusiasm of your presentation. You both are very versed on the subject matter and your commitment to each other and to your faith was uplifting."

"I really enjoyed the 'Daily Dozen' of stress—a much needed topic. Very practical advice and easy to apply."

"Foundational intimacies . . . has been something I've been thinking about and wanting to talk about with my spouse for years, and now finally have."

"It was well worth our time to participate. I'm sure it has opened up discussion and actions for us that will be very helpful to us in continuing to grow our relationship."

"I thought it was really good and practical information that a person could take and use."

"The effective merging of physiology and Christianity . . . For effective and applied Christian living this was very good."

"The talks on forgiveness were enlightening. I had not yet forgiven myself for a slight to my wife—although she had forgiven me . . . ."

"I like the therapy perspective—it is nice to know that problems in marriage can be resolved and not just eat away or split up the marriage."

Additional Resources From The Otrembas

- *A New Day in Christ: How to Calm Stress and Anxiety in 20 Minutes a Day*

- *Banquet of Love: The Eucharist as Weekly Marriage Enrichment*—DVD and workbook available

- *Celebrating the Sacraments of Reconciliation and First Eucharist*

To purchase these workbooks or to inquire about a workshop, visit:

www.healinginchrist.com
or
www.coachinginchrist.com

or email:

jimotremba@gmail.com
or
maureenotremba@gmail.com

Notes

Notes